Follow the Maker's Instructions

How to have the best in marriage and family life

Don and Heather Double

New Wine Press

New Wine Press
PO Box 17
Chichester
West Sussex PO20 6YB
England

First edition 1985.
Published by Marshall Pickering Communications.

ISBN: 1 874367 32 9

Typeset by CRB (Drayton) Typesetting Services, Norwich.
Printed in England by Clays Ltd, St Ives plc.

Acknowledgements

I am deeply grateful to Tim Jones for his commitment, hard work and dedication in producing this revised edition of *Follow the Maker's Instructions*. My thanks are also due to Peter Gammons who ghost-wrote the first edition for us.

Thanks to Gill Clarke who transcribed some of the tapes for the additional material and to Pat Darwood and David Reynolds for proof reading.

Also, many thanks to the Good News Crusade team, whose commitment and effort soaked up the added pressure during the weeks that Tim Jones was away writing the book.

Dedication

The first edition was dedicated to every marriage and family who have experienced any difficulties but have a desire to find an answer.

For this second edition we wish to add to that dedication.

Remembering our parents George and Lillian Double and John and Rhoda Martin who set us both examples of love and faithfulness to each other which we have been able to emulate.

Also our children Nigel, Julia, Stephen, Joel and Faith who have all been a joy to raise and have helped to make us what we are today.

Contents

PART THREE
Making a Family

PART FOUR
When Things Go Wrong

Foreword

I think that you will probably agree this is the best book on marriage you have ever read. It is punchy, down to earth, humorous, practical, helpful, and full of inspired common sense. My wife and I have recommended this book to many whether engaged, just married or married for a while. We have used it as the basis for a course on marriage in our church.

A strong marriage with God in the centre is a real power-house for the Kingdom of God and makes Satan tremble. Jesus says that when two or three agree on anything He is there in the midst. The ultimate partnership is a one-flesh union in marriage to your best friend, team worker, confidante and companion. When a man or woman 'go for it' together in God, committed to serving Him together, laying their lives before Him, then His power is released.

Marriage itself is a prophetic symbol of God's covenant with us, representing the relationship between Christ and the Church. It is a high calling and the stakes are high to get it right. In an era of AIDS it has never been more important for us to show the world a better way. Words are not enough: people need to see.

Good marriages require long term investment and hard work. They don't just fall out of the sky. Good marriages feed on taking time to communicate, on mutual respect, trust and understanding. Maybe you feel very happily married; then this book will show you how to share your joy so others can experience it too. Maybe you realise your marriage is not all it could be; then this book will help you to put it right.

In the age of AIDS it has never been clearer that if you want the best results from life, then you need to follow the instructions of the Maker. When we read the Bible we find a wonderful design for living which is physically healthy, emotionally satisfying, and spiritually fulfilling. This is the key to celebrating every day as a wonderful gift of God for us to enjoy with Him.

Dr Patrick Dixon
Medical Director
ACET (AIDS Care Education and Training)

Introduction

Have you ever bought a tool or kitchen appliance and started to use it having assumed that you knew how? A friend of mine did that with a new computerised typewriter. The machine was supposed to erase mistakes, but when she hit the erase key it did nothing but backspace. After getting frustrated she decided to look at the instruction book. It revealed that the typewriter was programmed somewhat differently than she had supposed. After learning what keys she should press she proceeded to type quite happily.

There is a right way and a wrong way to do everything. Many commercial products carry the caution, 'For the best results, follow the maker's instructions.' What is true for machinery also holds true for humans. If you want to get the best out of life, you are recommended to follow our Maker's instructions.

When God created this wonderful universe, it was not complete until man appeared (see Genesis 1 and 2). The first family God made should have lived in perfect harmony and happiness. In a sinless, beautiful earth, they really had it made. But what happened? They tried to do things their own way and everything, including their own relationship, very quickly deteriorated.

Throughout the history of mankind things have gone on the same way. Today, God's instructions are either unknown or ignored, and the result is chaos.

The family is the smallest unit of a nation, potentially the most important, and as a result it is under furious attack by governments, philosophers and ultimately demonic powers. Many people now look upon marriage as a convenience, a contract which can easily be broken if things do not go according to plan.

Nevertheless, the picture is not all bad. There are people today who are concerned about their families and are willing to take another look at the Maker's original designs. When men and women will do that, there is no limit to what God can do for them. As couples let Jesus be Lord in their lives, marriages and families, He is making them into something beautiful and satisfying.

In this second edition we have updated some parts and added several new chapters. The book has been written as a practical manual on marriage and family life. It seeks to explain God's original plans and to make it possible for you to easily apply them to your situation. We pray that as you do this, you will discover the joy and pleasure that comes from following the Maker's Instructions.

Don and Heather Double

PART ONE

The Recipe for a Happy Marriage

Chapter 1

Firm Foundations

Wedding Rings for Hire

The sign seen in a jeweller's shop window may have been a joke, but it is a sad reflection of a real situation in this country. The statistics show a rapid rise in the number of couples getting divorced, as are the figures for those who don't even bother getting married at all. Sadly, many people now regard marriage merely as a convenient agreement that can easily be broken.

Even Christians are not immune from the pressures that can lead to the breakdown of family life. However, God has not left us to struggle with these pressures alone. Marriage was not man's idea, it was and still is part of God's plan for humanity. Our Creator, the One who 'hung the stars in space', is intimately concerned for us. There is a vast amount of evidence for that fact. The Earth is perfectly positioned; if it were to move a fraction nearer to the Sun, we would all be burnt up, if it were to move the other way we would soon freeze to death. Everything that God does is perfect and we can take encouragement from that.

If you read the first two chapters of the book of Genesis two things are clear. God made us, and He designed us to enjoy the company of fellow humans.

> 'The LORD God said, "It is not good for the man to be alone. I will make a helper suitable for him." '
>
> (Genesis 2:18)

Therefore, we need to pay attention to what He says about living together, He knows what He is talking about!

Look in most bookshops and you will find lots of books about relationships and how to find security, fulfilment and happiness. Sociologists and psychologists and many other 'experts' are always ready with advice; there is a constant stream of new ideas on how to achieve the 'perfect relationship'. The problem is that if you look at the results of their teaching, you can find lots of hurting, disillusioned people. Heather and I have written this book because we have found that there is one book that is different, and can produce some very different results. The Bible is God's Word to mankind; think of it as the 'The Maker's Instructions', and if we follow them there is a guarantee of success. To disobey those instructions or ignore them will produce the results we can see all around us.

Many family problems are caused when family members do not take their God-ordained role. Our experience has been that tension and stress, which can lead to all kinds of physical sickness, are the result of problems in the family. Once, after Heather and I had taught on the subject of the family, a doctor came up to us. He said, 'If all my patients could hear what you have taught today, and were to put it into practice, it would cut down my daily surgery by half!'

The Blueprint

You have to build a good family. Like any other building programme, that means hard work and commitment to see the project finished. Good family relationships do not fall out of the sky! People sometimes say that marriages are made in heaven; I believe that the blueprints are, but the building work is done here on earth! Just because you have a blueprint, it does not follow that you will get the finished article. Just think about the building process:

> An architect must first of all see the building in his head. He puts it down on paper and then hands his

plans over to a builder, who should begin to build according to that design. The builder may involve various subcontractors in the work; with each of them he must explain the architect's intentions, so they can do their job correctly.

What happens if the builder does not follow the plans? If he gives each worker different plans, disaster will follow. The building will be different to what the architect designed and will probably be dangerous, even if it does not fall down immediately.

In the same way, marriages and family life have to be fashioned according to the specifications laid down by the Maker. They are found in His book, the Bible. Perhaps you feel that the Bible is an 'old-fashioned' book and not relevant to your life. The truth is that it is very relevant; there are parts of it that can tell you about the future with pinpoint accuracy. Human nature has not changed very much, if at all, since the Bible was written. As we study what it has to say about the subject of family life, I hope it will become evident to you just how helpful it can be.

Good marriages and families need working at, and take time. As you read the following pages, I believe that God will speak to you and highlight areas in your family's relationships that need adjustment. No matter how bad these relationships may be now, they can change if you are willing to follow God's instructions. All things are possible; you can enjoy your family, so remember that God is a God of miracles!

You may have read this far and think that your marriage is OK and there are no problems. That is great, but please read on. Be encouraged about the things that you are doing right, but be ready for God to point out the areas where there is room for improvement. As we bring our lives more into line with the Word of God and better understand those 'Instructions', we will find greater fulfilment and blessing in family life.

Laying the Foundations

The strength of any building depends on the depth and firmness of its foundations. Family life is the same. In one well-known parable Jesus spoke about two builders. One man built on rocky ground and the other on sand (Matthew 7:24–26). Jesus compared the two builders and emphasised the ground they chose to build on. When the storms came, the house built on the rock survived, while the house on the sand collapsed. Why? The foundations on the sand gave way under the pressure of the storm.

Jesus went on to say,

> *'Everyone who hears these words of mine and does not put them into practice is like a foolish man who built his house on sand. The rain came down, the streams rose, and the winds blew and beat against that house, and it fell with a great crash.'* (Matthew 7:26–27)

It is not enough to find out what God's instructions are, we must put them into practice. Being a Christian is no guarantee of a successful marriage. If we do not put God's principles into action we are as vulnerable as anyone else.

The finest illustration I know for building a husband and wife relationship is that of a triangle. Picture the husband on one side, the wife on the other, and God at the top. A successful marriage starts with the husband and wife each seeking to get as close to God as possible. They may start some distance apart from each other, but as they each move 'up the triangle', getting closer to God, something else happens. They also come into a closer and more intimate relationship with each other. The emphasis and direction of growth are God-ward, not man-ward, and yet the result is a unity of heart and mind that comes from the Spirit of God Himself.

Beginning the Work

The first foundation for a successful life is to surrender and totally give our lives to the Lord Jesus Christ. It is really only when this foundation is laid, that the other foundations we will consider in this book can work.

In the book of Genesis we read of an amazing man, Enoch. It says of him,

> '*After he became the father of Methuselah, Enoch walked with God 300 years and had other sons and daughters.*'   (Genesis 5:22)

Here is a family man, a most outstanding character in the Bible, a man who walked with God for three hundred years! You may think that if Enoch was in your family, he could never have kept such a testimony. The truth is that even with a wife and several children, Enoch still walked with the Lord. I have a wife and five children so I am not just talking about an ideal theory. I know what the pressures and strains of family life are like, but that should not hinder our relationship with God.

Jesus said '*no one will take away your joy*' (John 16:22). If your joy has gone and you have lost the sense of God's closeness, the offender is not your spouse or your child; you cannot blame anyone but yourself. True, others may be involved, but ultimately, it is you who is responsible for your own walk. Each member of the family needs to have a personal relationship with the Lord. A really successful family life flows from each member's communion with God. Everything worth having in the Christian life comes from this relationship. What sort of communion does your family have with God? Are you maintaining a day to day, real relationship with Him?

Families are a vitally important part of church life. Activities like Bible Study, prayer and worshipping together are all important but so are our responsibilities to the family. I often meet people who think that they ought to be out, working in their church, and so they neglect their families. That is wrong. Some people have the idea that if the church is right, their family will be right, but this is getting things in the wrong order.

The Apostle Paul's letter to the Ephesians illustrates my point very well. The whole letter is concerned with Church, and the ways a church should function. Right in the middle of that letter, in the centre of his teaching about church life, what do we read? Instructions to husbands and wives, children and parents!

There is one church that I have regularly visited over a period of years. At one point the members started to enter a new depth of relationship with each other. They deliberately began to spend time 'building' with each other. Sometime after this had started, I was sitting in their service waiting to preach. I could see that there was something different from what I had experienced there over the previous ten years. They had become a family, they were relaxed and enjoying each other, and the Lord. That can never happen in a church until it has happened in the families that comprise it.

What goes on in the family, affects the church. If there is tension in the family, you will take the tension to the church meetings with you. When there is friction in the home, you will take that friction into church. The Church will always be short of leaders when husbands are not right and in God's order in the family. If wives are not submitted to their husbands, members of the church will struggle to submit to each other. If children do not obey their parents, the church will be undisciplined.

This is one reason why there is so little power and effectiveness in most churches. People pretend to be one thing when the church meets together on Sunday morning, but they behave very differently for the rest of the week at home. As family life breaks down around us, there is no greater witness for the Lord than families who are wholeheartedly living for the Lord and for each other. God wants us to be models of what family life should be, in a world that is crying out for answers.

Down to Earth

Once we have established that first foundation of submitting to Jesus Christ we can move on. The next foundation is to give ourselves totally and unreservedly to our partner. A true marriage demands a complete commitment to each other. As you read this book, decide that you will work out together the things that God speaks to you about.

In the book of Ecclesiastes there is a proverb:

'A cord of three strands is not quickly broken.'
(Ecclesiastes 4:12)

As we look at family relationships, and particularly the one between husband and wife, remember the triangle I talked about earlier. The three strands – you, your partner and God – woven together to make one tough 'cord'.

When we involve God in our lives, we can truly enjoy marriage. His instructions are so clear; the various roles and functions He has ordained for us do work!

As we begin to look at the instructions God has given, there are three steps that will help you get the most out of this book:

1. As you read, ask the Lord to have His way in your life. Be open for Him to speak to you and change you, in any way He wants. Without this attitude, reading this book would be a waste of time. God is always right, and to fight against Him is pointless. The truth is we need God's radical surgery to be whole; we are totally incapable of working things out 'our way'.

    If you find yourself arguing with God about what He is saying, the best action is to get before Him and ask Him to change you. Don't try to ignore Him. Charles Finney defined repentance as 'Giving up all controversy with God and admitting He is totally right on every point and that the sinner is totally wrong.'

2. Expect God to speak to **you**. Do not 'pitchfork' things onto your partner thinking 'This is just what they need

to hear.' It is not your job to change your partner or family. If they need to change, the best thing that you can do is pray for them. As you read, make sure that you are fulfilling your role correctly, and doing everything God is asking of you.

3. Be open and talk about the things that God is saying to you. I suggest that you study this book together as a husband and wife, or even as a family. Discuss what you read, pray about issues and work them out together.

Before we go any further, please stop and pray.

If you know you don't have a living relationship with God do something about it today. If you are ready to go on and discover the Maker's Instructions pray:

'Heavenly Father, you know all about me. I acknowledge that You created me and You have a perfect plan for my life, my marriage, my family. As I read the instructions You have given, please speak to me. I want to be obedient to You and get the best for my marriage and family. I pray that You would help put right the things that are wrong, and improve those areas where things are OK but could be better. Don't let me get away with anything Lord, I want Your best. In Jesus' name, Amen.'

Chapter 2

Husbands and Headship

> *'Wives, submit to your husbands as to the Lord. For the husband is the head of the wife as Christ is the head of the church, his body, of which he is the Saviour. Now as the church submits to Christ, so also wives should submit to their husbands in everything. Husbands, love your wives, just as Christ loved the church and gave himself up for her.'*   (Ephesians 5:22–25)

Every husband should be the leader in his own household. By household, I mean a man, his wife, children and any others who are living under his roof. The Bible says that a husband is the head of his wife. He does not have to earn this position, or ask his wife's permission, nor does he have to 'become' the head, because God has already put him there. God has anointed him to fulfil that role.

You may say, 'My wife has a stronger personality and is far more gifted; she is more a leader than I am.' While her gifts may be different to yours, both of you need to accept God's plan for you. He has placed every husband in the position of headship, and has given him the ability to lead his family. He is the one who takes final responsibility for what his family becomes and the one who should provide security in the home.

Every husband needs to take his place as the head of his wife. Some men say to me, 'But my wife will not submit.'

Very often, the reason she will not submit is that her husband will not take up his proper responsibilities as the head and lead. This is both a tragedy and dishonouring to God.

God did not make *'man for woman, but woman for man'* (1 Corinthians 11:9). He designed us according to His plan and as the One who made us we need to pay attention to what He says.

> *'Now I want you to realize that the head of every man is Christ, and the head of the woman is man, and the head of Christ is God.'* (1 Corinthians 11:3)

This is God's 'chain of command'. God has ordained and declared that the husband is the head. A husband does not have to ask his wife for permission to be the head; he is already.

If a husband wants his wife to be in biblical submission and respect his headship he must show her that Christ is his head. The wife must see how her husband submits to Christ so she can learn how to submit to him. In other words the husband should be a model of submission for his wife to follow.

Follow Jesus

> *'I am able to do nothing from myself – independently, of my own accord – but am taught by God and as I get his orders, (I decide as I am bidden to decide. As the voice comes to me, so I give a decision.) Even as I hear, I judge and my judgement is right (just, righteous), because I do not seek or consult my own will – I have no desire to do what is pleasing to myself, my own aim, my own purpose – but only the will and pleasure of the Father who sent me.'* (John 5:30 The Amplified Bible)

What a perfect example of submission to authority and headship!

Headship is a responsibility; a responsibility which husbands need to accept and work out. In our society there is an attitude of 'passing the buck'. No one wants to take responsibility for anything; if you can avoid it, you are doing well. Men of God should be different. Are you willing to take responsibility? Are you willing for the 'buck' to stop with you?

As she sees her husband develop a relationship with Jesus, a godly wife will readily submit to her husband. It will not be difficult, she will want to do it, because she will find security in her relationship with her husband, knowing he loves her. Our responsibility as the head is to love our wives as Christ loved the Church and gave Himself for it. This kind of love is sadly very rare today; it is the kind of love that allowed Jesus Christ to lay down His life for the Church. Are you willing to lay down your life for your wife? It will mean a sacrificial giving of yourself to your wife, working out your headship by loving and serving her.

Many husbands refuse or avoid being head, and it has disastrous effects on the family. If you opt out of your responsibilities are you aware of the consequences? Do you realise you can affect the physical health of your wife and children? Insecurity, tension and stress, migraines, psychiatric problems and even nervous breakdowns can all be the result of a husband not being head. This is very serious and you need to know that, one day, you will have to give an account to the Lord for what your family becomes.

Being the head does not mean that the husband is superior to his wife, neither does it mean he is better. God who made them both has designed them for specific roles. Only as both partners move in their God-given roles can they find fulfilment.

Family Devotions

As head, a husband is responsible for the spiritual welfare of his family.

There is much truth in the statement, 'The family that

prays together, stays together.' Do not leave it to your wife to assume the position of 'priest' in your home. If you think she is more spiritual than you, then you need to seek God and decide, by His grace, to change things. When you show you are willing to take the lead, your wife will probably be relieved and gladly give you space to function.

When Heather and I went on our honeymoon, the first thing we did when we arrived, was to kneel by our bed and pray together. I thank God that we laid that foundation from the beginning, and we still seek to pray together every day. As our family has grown up, we have endeavoured each day, after the evening meal, to have a devotional time. We usually pray and read a portion from God's Word. Even when they were very small, every member of the family took part; it is beautiful to see the simple faith and expectancy of a young child's prayers. In our home, spending time with the Lord together has naturally become a part of our life together.

When we first started a devotional time, we began by praying, around the table, one at a time. Eventually it became quite spontaneous and we learnt as a family to really 'pray through' issues. Sometimes the gifts of the Spirit were used, or we would have a time of worship. After we read a passage from Scripture, we would each share what the Lord said to us through it.

Husbands, it is your responsibility to arrange family devotions. They should be exciting, a time that the family look forward to. If they are regarded as a chore something is wrong. It is important to keep them varied, so if you need help there are a number of very good 'family devotional' books available.

Whenever we faced a crisis as a family, we talked and prayed about it at these devotional times. A situation may seem to be insurmountable to the parents, but when taken and shared with the whole family, someone may bring a fresh perspective no one had seen. In Galatians 6:2 it says, *'bear one another's burdens,'* and the whole family can do that together. As they then unite in faith together, faith will grow as God moves in the situation.

When Stephen was sixteen and approaching the time to leave school, he felt strongly that he wanted a job in banking. We all agreed in prayer about this and he wrote to the local banks. However, he received the same reply from them all, 'Not yet. We are not employing any school leavers this year.' Each bank suggested that he should attend college and take a BEC course and then reapply in two years' time. However, we refused to accept defeat as we strongly believed that God was saying otherwise, and we continued to pray. He then went for an interview with another bank and was immediately offered a job.

Back at school the Careers Officer asked him what he wanted to do on leaving school. He informed them that he had already got a job in a local bank. They told him that he must be mistaken, and could only have an interview. They refused to believe that he had actually got a job as so many pupils had applied for jobs in the bank and had been told that none were available.

Each family needs to find their own identity and flow as God leads them in their devotional times. 'Devotions' do not need to be long but every member of the family should be involved; this includes extended family and anyone staying in your home. Do not leave it to the Sunday School to train your children; it is your job. It is while sitting on your knee that they should learn about the Gospel.

> 'Hear, O Israel: The LORD our God, the LORD is one. Love the LORD your God with all your heart and with all your soul and with all your strength. These commandments that I give you today are to be upon your hearts. Impress them on your children. Talk about them when you sit at home and when you walk along the road, when you lie down and when you get up.'
>
> (Deuteronomy 6:4–7)

Once I stayed in a home where the whole family was

converted, except the husband. He was a director of a big company and a very influential man. On the first night of my stay he heard me preach on the subject of family devotions. Later as we were discussing how important it was to pray together, he quite unexpectedly, got up and with real emotion gripped my hand. He then took the hand of another member of the family and said, 'Let's start now.' It was a beginning and on the last night of my stay in his house he was wonderfully saved.

Husbands, lead your family in everything, especially in spiritual matters. Be an example to your children. If you don't have family devotions it will take discipline to start, but there is no better or easier time to begin than today.

Where Now?

Headship also means giving direction to the family. So many marriages drift into routine and become dead, dry and formal. Marriage should be exciting, and can be if the husband brings direction. When was the last time that you led your family into something new, something that you had never done before? I challenge you, get alone with God and He will give you direction.

When Heather and I counsel couples, we often hear the complaint that their marriage has become stale and boring. At the time of writing Heather and I have been married for thirty years and we still find it exciting as we grow and develop in our relationship. With the Lord's help we believe that our marriage will get better yet.

Only as Christ was subject to the Father was He able to fulfil His Father's will. In the same way, only as a man is himself subject to Christ, can he fulfil Christ's will as far as his family is concerned. The Centurion who came to Jesus said,

> 'For I myself am a man under authority, with soldiers under me. I tell this one, "Go," and he goes; and that

> *one, "Come," and he comes. I say to my servant, "Do*
> *this," and he does it.'*   (Matthew 8:9)

His authority came from being under Caesar's authority. Our authority as husbands comes from being under the Lord's. When a husband is under Christ's lordship there is an automatic flow of divine authority.

Headship not Lordship

The husband's authority does not come by lording it over his wife. God does not want a dictator in the home; He is calling us to lead by serving and Jesus gave us the example. *'The greatest among you will be your servant'* (Matthew 23:11). I would never ask Heather to do something that is not good for her; she knows that and so it is easy for her to submit. Submission does not mean that she cannot share with me if she feels that I am wrong.

I remember one occasion when I had decided to do something which I was convinced God wanted me to do. Heather did not know what I was planning, but she discovered it in a letter that came for us while I was away. She wrote a little note on the back of the envelope when she sent it on to me. 'Are you sure this is right? Do you remember that when we got married, God gave us a prophecy and He said...?' That was the voice of God to me! I heard God through my wife and it was then my turn to submit to God.

God has given you a wife to help you (Genesis 2:18). If you resist that help, you will miss so much of what God has for you. This does not mean that you should be easily manipulated or emotionally blackmailed into making decisions against your better judgement. We need to grow beyond manipulation. However, do not get hardhearted; even if your loved one sins by seeking to manipulate you, it is no reason to hurt her.

There is an important place for talking things through and hearing your wife's mind when making decisions. We are to lead our families, not drive them. God wants the husband to be a leader who leads by love and by example. I learnt this lesson when I became aware of a problem in Stephen's life. As I was getting ready to deal with it I talked to the Lord. His reply was a shock because He said to me, 'It's your problem, not Stephen's.' 'What do you mean, Lord? He is doing this.' The Lord then said, 'Yes, but look at yourself.' I did and had to repent. It was not necessary to say a word to Stephen because within two or three days he changed. If you want to know what you are like, look at your children! You are a leader and they will follow you, even in the bad points.

Be a man of your word. If you say you'll do something, do it, because if you don't, you are lying and in sin. How do you expect your children to believe you, when you tell them God's Word is true and that He keeps His promises, if you break yours? The practical outworking of this truth may well mean that you have to discipline yourself to do the jobs you have been putting off.

Heart Submission

It is a sure recipe for disaster if you start saying to your wife, 'You have to submit to me.' Your part is to obey the Bible's instruction to husbands, and to take up your responsibilities. Her part is to obey God's instructions to wives.

Too many husbands are following their wives or children and as a result the Church is bereft of leaders. The Bible makes it clear that the husband cannot properly play his role in the Church if his family is not in order.

> *'If anyone does not know how to manage his own family, how can he take care of God's church?'* (1 Timothy 3:5)

In fact, if your relationship with your wife isn't right, your whole prayer life and relationship with God is affected:

> *'Husbands, in the same way be considerate as you live with your wives, and treat them with respect as the*

> *weaker partner and as heirs with you of the gracious gift*
> *of life, so that nothing will hinder your prayers.'*
>
> (1 Peter 3:7)

God gives you the authority to be the head in your household. You do not have to work at it or attain to it because you have it! If you ask any member of my family who has the authority they won't hesitate to reply. But ask them how much authority I wield, and the answer will be 'hardly any'. I do not need to throw my weight around. Authority is like soap, the more you use it – the less you have!

If you have not been taking the lead before, repent and ask your wife to forgive you. By God's grace start leading your family today. Give your family the security of knowing that they have a head.

Cherish Your Wife

When you got married, if you used the 'traditional' vows, you made a promise to cherish your wife. Are you aware of what you committed yourself to do? Do you know what the word means? I did a study on 'cherish' and came up with the following definitions:

To Cherish:

To love

To hold dear

To revere

To treasure

To value

To praise

To appreciate

To venerate

To honour

To protect

To esteem

To idolize

To nurse

To nourish

To nurture

To sustain

To shelter

To care for

To tend lovingly

To keep in one's heart

To cling to

Are you keeping your promise? I believe that when God made woman, He put something in her that needs and responds to being cherished. This list of activities is a challenge; if you set a goal to cherish your wife in these ways not only will you have a happy wife, you will discover the true help God has given you. You will also find a person who is willing to follow you to 'the ends of the earth'.

Chapter 3

Which One?

A couple were once heard to say, 'We were told that when we got married we became one. Ever since then, we have been arguing about which of us is the one!'

God wants a husband and wife to be whole as a couple. He wants us to be one. God is a triune (three part) being, Father, Son and Holy Spirit, and He made us in His image. He made us triune beings: body, soul and spirit. For us to be whole, we have to be whole in each of these areas. To be whole as couples, we have to be rightly related to each other in body, soul and spirit.

One in Body

When a couple marry and relate together physically they become one flesh. This is very natural, and God wants us to enjoy our sexual relationship. Any idea to the contrary, regarding sex to be something evil, unclean or unnecessary is of the devil. God created the sexual relationship. He made sex so that we could have children, but He also made it for our enjoyment.

One in Spirit

A problem in many marriages is that the couple are unequally yoked. Some people consider this as solely describing a Christian married to a non-Christian. This, of course, is bound to cause problems. However, I believe that being unequally yoked is equally applicable when one partner is baptized in the Holy Spirit and the other is not, or when husband and wife belong to different churches.

A couple should pray together, worship together, and serve together in every aspect of their lives. Their spiritual goals should be the same. For Heather and me a very significant point in our relationship came when we decided that our goals and desires for the Kingdom of God in our lives needed to be joined. The result has been a wonderful agreement in spiritual things; often God will speak to each of us about something and when we confer there is a wonderful unity in what we have heard. At a conference some while ago we split into two groups; the men were with me and the women were in another room with Heather. We gave everyone a passage from the Bible to meditate on for a short time to see what God would show us. It was a marvellous time. The Lord showed me things I had never seen before, even to the extent that I was a little concerned because I thought it might be controversial. When we went to the breakfast table, I shared these thoughts with Heather. She said, 'That is wonderful. God showed me the same thing. I was the only one who had this, and blessed the others by it.'

Once when I was in Chile God shared something with me, so I wrote home and shared it with Heather. By the time she got the letter, she had already written to me saying the very same thing. God had already spoken to her about it, although we were several thousand miles apart.

Both these examples illustrate one of the goals that God wants a husband and wife to enjoy – to be spiritually 'in tune' with each other. I never entertain the idea that Heather and I are anything but one in spirit. We never consider ourselves as two individuals. Although we have different personalities, God has put us together to make us whole.

One in Soul

Have you noticed how a husband and wife can flow in the Spirit together during the Sunday morning service? For example, the husband brings a message in tongues and the wife gives the interpretation. Yet an hour later they are arguing over a mundane thing like getting the lunch ready. How can this be? They have never learned to relate where it really counts, in the soul realm. In Acts 4:32 we are told that the Church was *'of one heart and one soul and with great power gave the apostles' witness to the resurrection of the Lord Jesus.'* What was the key to their effectiveness? It was not just because they were of one heart but because they were of one soul too! They had learnt to relate soul to soul.

The soul consists of the will, the mind and the emotions. Until we are willing to open our lives and build together in these areas we will never be truly one. Sadly some couples live together for sixty or more years, having never become truly one in their souls.

The Will

Have you ever said of your partner, 'They have a will of their own?' Well, that statement may be true, but God wants us to become one in our will. This never happens easily or painlessly, but it is possible.

Heather loves archaeology and looking at historical sites, a subject that I struggle with. I love nature and so it is not difficult to see how easily a disagreement could arise. 'I want to see the wildlife park', 'Well, I want to see the castle.' There does need to be mutual submission in our hearts and the truth is that selfishness is responsible for such disharmony. When my heart is right, I can do things that I would not choose to do, because I want to please Heather. What is more, I make sure my attitude is 'I am going to enjoy myself, not just to endure it like a martyr.'

It is possible for a couple to be one in will. I used to hate going shopping. Now I love it and I do not like Heather to go without me, because God has changed me. I used to feel like a dog on a lead, looking in the windows. 'Do you like this one? Do you like that one?' That changed when I opened my heart and asked God to change me.

What do you do when two strong wills are involved? Those who know Heather and me, know that we are both strong-willed people. The only answer to a strong will is submission. Ephesians 5:21 says *'Submit yourselves to one another.'* Until we disagree it is difficult to prove we are truly in submission. Mutual submission is a key to becoming one in will.

Look at Jesus. When He was in the Garden of Gethsemane, He showed us the perfect way. He prayed,

> *'O My Father, if it is possible, let this cup pass from Me, nevertheless, not as I will, but as You will.'*
>
> (Matthew 26:39 NKJV)

This shows us that the Son in His humanity, had a will separate from His Father's will. The Bible tells us that Jesus only did the things that His Father showed Him to do. This teaches us how our will should be. He never demanded his own way. If He had done His own thing, by acting independently, He would have been incapable of redeeming us. That is how serious it is. In everything He submitted to His Father's will.

We see the depth of this truth in Jesus' words, in John 5:30 in the Amplified Bible:

> *'I am able to do nothing from Myself – independently, of my own accord – but as I am taught by God **and** as I get His orders. [I decide as I am bidden to decide. As the voice comes to Me, so I give a decision.] Even as I hear, I judge and My judgement is right [just, righteous] because I do not seek **or** consult My own will – I have no desire to do what is pleasing to Myself, My own aim, My*

*own purpose – but only the will **and** pleasure of the Father Who sent Me.'*

'*Christ did not please Himself*' (Romans 15:3). That should be the goal in our relationship together. Have we come to the place where we are prepared to lay our wills down?

The Mind

Education, theology and our upbringing all shape our thinking. So often, when two minds get together they think differently and **boom!** There is an explosion!

Our minds need renewing. We must recognize that it is God who has called us together, and commit ourselves to becoming all that He wants us to be. Once we have made that commitment we will begin to hear Him saying the same thing. However, this is not uniformity but harmony, as one complements the other. 'What she has is mine and what I have is hers.'

Heather is academically bright, but due to tuberculosis in my formative years, I missed a great deal of schooling and so have had difficulty reading and writing. However, because we are one, I do not feel inferior, nor does Heather feel superior. Together there is a beautiful harmony. What Heather has, she has given to me. When she said in our marriage vows 'With all my worldly goods I thee endow,' she gave herself to me. She gave her educated mind to me, and so we work together. I do not feel a failure in this area, because together we are one. For example, I will often work out what I want in a letter, and she does the writing and the spelling. (When I am away and write to Heather she needs the gift of interpretation to understand it!) Yet, together we complement each other and can be an effective unit.

The Emotions

Finally, we need to look at the realm of the emotions. Many

Christians hold some extremely strange ideas about their emotions. Some say, 'You must not be emotional when you go to Church,' but that implies I should leave my soul behind! The Bible tells us that the elders have to watch over our souls (Hebrews 13:17 NKJV). If I leave my soul at home, it would be difficult for them to do their job!

Many couples cannot weep or laugh together. The Lord wants to melt our hearts so that we can weep in His presence. Jesus saw the state of men and women and was moved to compassion. In the same way, we need to be touched with compassion for one another's infirmities. Very often one partner cannot feel how the other feels because of a hard heart. If this describes you, please get before the Lord so that He can soften it. God gave us our emotions for a purpose.

Tears are very precious to the Lord. I cannot think of anyone more emotional than the woman who washed Jesus' feet with her tears and dried them with her hair. He did not condemn her but said,

> *'Leave her alone ... Wherever the Gospel is preached throughout the world, what she has done will also be told, in memory of her.'* (Mark 14:6–9)

We must be totally open with each other and come to the place where we can truly share our thoughts and feelings. *'Perfect love drives out fear'* (1 John 4:18), so if there is love between us, we should not threaten each other. I should be free to say anything without threatening my partner or being afraid of what she says. If we really love each other there is no need to wear masks, pretending to be something we are not.

Emotional Hang-ups

When someone is feeling down, 'one degree under', it often affects the way they react. We need to let our partner into our lives, so that they will know how we really feel.

Otherwise, they can get frustrated when we don't respond in the way they expect. Learning to share your emotions will help develop sensitivity in your relationship. We all have a different emotional make-up. It takes time to understand our partner's emotions.

Together we can blend to make a whole, but this is very different from trying to be carbon copies of each other. Although we are all different emotionally, I do not believe that one person should be dominant, particularly in lovemaking for example. Many people feel restricted and unable to express themselves. The truth is, we are made in the image of God. He is always able to express Himself clearly and this is how He wants us to be. I want to look at four major causes of people becoming emotionally stifled.

Childhood hurts

I meet many people who as children wanted to be loved, but were pushed aside by one or both of their parents. This has caused a fear of expressing themselves in case they get hurt again. One manifestation of this hurt that I often see is that one or both partners relate together in sexual lust, instead of genuine love. The sex act is used for self gratification, rather than as an opportunity to give. This will, of course, lead to many problems, because lust never lasts. The answer is to come before the Lord so that He can heal those hurts. (It may be necessary to use professional help in this process.)

Ignorance

Heather and I counsel many people with marriage difficulties. It is amazing how frequently we discover that a lack of affection between a husband and wife goes back to a problem they experienced as children. Many children never see their parents express any physical affection for each other in front of them. As those children grow into adulthood they learn to suppress any feelings of love they have and do not express them. Parents must feel free to show their children that an open display of affection for

41

each other is normal. Parents, you are the most important model to your children of what love is – make sure that they see love that is normal, wholesome and expressive.

Cultural background

'British reserve', the 'stiff upper-lip' syndrome, is both ungodly and unbiblical. I encourage you to read the Song of Solomon, understanding that it is an account of two lovers expressing themselves to each other. This should then release you into a new dimension of expressing yourself physically and emotionally to your partner. You may not consider yourself a great poet or writer, but at least try to find new words to express your feelings. It may take effort at first, but it will be worth it in the end.

Guilt complex

Brian and Christine were in their early twenties and had been dating, on and off, for about five years. I knew them both very well and wanted their relationship to succeed. One night in a meeting I noticed how disheartened Christine looked. I went to her after the meeting and asked what was wrong. A very curt 'Nothing' was all I got. I looked her in the eyes and said, 'You know me better than to give an answer like that.' At which point it all came out. They had broken up, again, because they couldn't cope sexually, and had gone further than they should.

As we talked, she affirmed that they felt that they were right for each other. They loved each other very much, but they thought that their strong sexual desires must be wrong. I told her that it was perfectly normal for two human beings in such a relationship to feel this way for each other. It would concern me if they didn't! As Paul said,

> *'It is better to marry than burn with passion.'*
> (1 Corinthians 7:9)

She left me with a new release. After talking it through with

Brian they were engaged within a month and a year later they were married.

Guilt makes a person unable to understand what a healthy desire actually is and also prevents the practise of self-control. Pre-marital or extramarital sex, homosexuality or lesbianism will all produce guilt. That guilt will emotionally stifle a person so that they cannot express themselves properly. The cause of many marriage problems is guilt from past sins that have been suppressed and hidden. It is so important to repent and get things into the light with each other, ideally before you marry. If you are already married, be very sensitive and prayerful about the right time to confess, but do it.

All sexual relationships outside marriage are sinful. If a person commited fornication (pre-marital sex) before they married, either with their future spouse or with someone else, it will affect their whole marriage. Their ability to trust each other, not just about sex, will be affected. Sadly I counsel too many Christians who struggle with the consequences of this sin for many years before they get free. All fornication is sin, even if the couple eventually do get married. They need to repent and believe that the blood of Jesus will cleanse their sin. Marriage does not legalise the sin of pre-marital sex. If you and your partner committed fornication, however long ago, and are now married, you both need to repent.

Fornication and adultery, even if it is just a 'one-off', is more than an act that happens once and is then forgotten. Something happens between the two individuals that has a spiritual dimension. That is why Paul says in 1 Corinthians 6:16:

> *'Do you not know that he who unites himself with a prostitute is one with her in body? For it is said, "The two will become one flesh."'*

Two becoming one flesh has been described as a 'soul-tie'. However you describe the result, any sexual relationship that occurred outside the commitment of marriage needs dealing with, or it will cause damage. The answer is honest confession and repentance. Praise God for the abundant forgiveness that is found in Jesus Christ.

It is possible to be one in mind, will and emotions. To get there will require a mutual submission to each other. There will probably need to be repentance from wrong thoughts, desires, and emotional responses. Building soul to soul should be a major priority with your partner. It is also important with other members of your family and with brothers and sisters in the church too. What sort of testimony is it to the world when they see Christians criticising, backbiting, and losing their tempers? As we have seen, it is in the soul realm where the 'grating' often takes place. With almost everyone I have sought to build with soul to soul, it has been painful. It is hard work but worth it.

Chapter 4

Communication

When it comes to communication Heather and I have still got our 'L' plates on. We have made tremendous progress over the years but we are still improving. It does not matter how long you have been married, I believe there are still things to learn about communication. Often when communication breaks down, that is when our problems start. I think that if we could perfect our communication skills we would get close to perfect marriages.

God is the perfect communicator; He sent Jesus to express to us what He is like. Our heavenly Father wants a relationship with people and so He sent His one and only Son, Jesus, to communicate with us.

> *'But if we walk in the light, as he is in the light, we have fellowship with one another, and the blood of Jesus, his Son, purifies us from all sin.'* (1 John 1:7)

Take a hard look at your marriage and you will soon see that most husband/wife problems start here. If we walk in the light, as He is in the light, we have fellowship one with another. If we don't walk in the light, fellowship with one another is hindered. We can paraphrase that verse and say 'If we don't communicate with each other, our relationship will falter.' A principle I work by, and often tell people is that

God works in the light, Satan works in the darkness.

I am determined to stay in the light as much as I can and will bring every situation into the light of God's word whenever I can.

A friend of mine once spent some time meditating on this verse from 1 John. His conclusion was that God cannot discover anything about him, because He already knows it all. God knows everything there is to know about me and you. That means there is nothing that will ever surprise Him. He knows the end from the beginning. There is nothing hidden from Him at all.

John tells us to walk in the light in the same measure that God is in the light. This means that we have got to become so open and so honest with one another as husband and wife, that we cannot discover anything new about each other! It means that there will be no secrets hidden from our partners. If you are honest, you know there are nearly always things that you are hiding from each other (and I am not talking about what you have bought as a birthday present!)

So, we need to open ourselves up and begin to share our thoughts, feelings and emotions with each other. It is a wonderful source of security when we achieve that. Also, it is much easier for you to tell your wife something, than for somebody else to tell her, or for her to find out another way. We need to make sure there are absolutely no 'no-go' areas in our lives. My goal is to let Heather into every area of my life; in the same way, I want to get into every area of her life. It is only at this point that we will discover the real depth and strength of our marriage.

Breaking the Barriers

Heather and I took a long time and some hard work to get to this place. We had been married for about ten years and had a good marriage. But 'good' is often the enemy of 'best'. I don't want just a good marriage – I want the best marriage.

Some people had invited me to speak in their church in Penzance and Heather came with me. As we drove and began to talk, I started to explain why I couldn't be open with her about some issues. The reason was that I was afraid of her reactions. Heather then told me about some areas she was afraid to talk to me about for the same reason. It was a great day for our marriage because we began to deal with the barriers that were keeping us apart.

Ask yourself this question: If you told your partner something about yourself which you thought would upset them, what do you do? All of us have to deal with the 'fear of reaction' – the volcano might erupt, or they may go quiet or even walk out. It is at this point that we discover how much trust there is between us.

Bridges of Trust

As a married couple we need to develop a relationship grounded on trust. I'm sure that you have seen signs on the side of the road warning of a bridge ahead that has a 10-tonne weight limit. The sign tells you that you would be unwise to drive a 30-tonne truck over it.

The process of building a relationship involves making a bridge of trust. As the relationship grows, the bridge is strengthened and we can communicate at a deeper level. Our goal as a couple should be to build a bridge that is so strong that we can 'drive' anything over it. What does that mean? Simply, that whatever you discover about your partner, however bad or horrible, you will not react badly and you will work through the issue. It does not mean you will be untouched by what is said, but that you will handle it in a way that allows communication to continue.

The conversation Heather and I had on the way to Penzance was difficult to start but the fruit was wonderful. Our relationship and love for each other was strengthened as we shared and brought the light into those hidden corners.

Feeling the Way

Good communication involves more than words. All of us, especially women, rely on our feelings. They affect our judgement and how we react to situations. As a husband I am committed to find out what Heather is feeling, not just listen to the facts that she speaks. I need to know what she feels about issues, because I have learnt to value her 'feminine intuition'. There are several occasions when I have thought, 'I wish I had taken more notice of Heather; she was right in what she felt.' Often it has taken months, sometimes even years, for me to recognise a problem that she had a 'hunch' about.

Learn to respect each other in this. We are made differently and God uses those differences as He communicates with us. Husbands, learn to be sensitive and allow your wife's feelings to come through with her words. I have learnt that when Heather says 'I can't put this into words, but I feel...' I need to pay attention. I used to be very different, and dismiss her feelings as just feminine weakness, but I have learnt the hard way that they are valuable to me.

Commandment Number 11

A member of my team has suggested that Moses missed a commandment; God intended eleven not ten! The eleventh commandment should be 'Thou shalt not make assumptions.'

It may be a fanciful story, but it has an important truth if we want to communicate better. Never assume that when you say something, your partner has heard what you have said. Also, don't assume that you have heard something completely at the first go. We have become so sophisticated that we think that communication happens perfectly every time. The truth is that a large part of what we say is not heard. We have got to stop assuming it is. Do you recognise this conversation?

'I told you ... '

'No you didn't.'

'Yes I did.'

'No, you never told me that.'

'I can remember where we were and what you were doing when I told you.'

'I'm sorry but you have never said that to me at all. I always remember things like that.'

I am sure that I am not the only one who has such debates. We need to recognise that just because we say something it does not mean our listeners have heard us.

God got through to me on this issue in a Church Elders' meeting. We were talking about a problem that was affecting the church. The other elders were discussing what to do about it, but I sat there very puzzled. As they continued talking, I interjected 'I don't understand. No one should have a problem with this, because I have preached about it in the church.' Their reply opened my eyes, 'Don, you don't think that because you preached it, they heard you, do you?'

On several occasions Jesus said *'He who has ears, let him hear'* (Matthew 13:9). Jesus knew that communication was more than saying words. He knew it was more than just talking, and more than just hearing, it involves 'active listening'. Sometimes, if it is an important matter, I will get Heather to tell me what she has heard me say. That way, I know that what I wanted to say has got over. She's not always pleased when I do that, but often there is no alternative.

Hearing is not Listening

One problem I am working to overcome often happens after I have preached. Somebody will come up and start talking to me. As they speak, I am trying to listen, but also find myself looking around to see what else is going on in the meeting. I might be listening but I am not concentrating. Unfortunately, I also communicate 'Don is not really

49

interested in me.' I have to make an effort to listen properly. In that setting it means fixing my eyes on the speaker until they have finished talking.

I used to do the same thing at home and it would really annoy Heather. She would start to talk to me but would know my attention was on something else. I would suddenly 'click' back as I heard, 'You haven't heard a word I have said.' We had to work this through. For us, when Heather wants to talk to me about something important, she will say 'Don I want to speak to you and I want your undivided attention. Tell me when we can sit and talk.' We are both very busy people and so to achieve it, we will sometimes have to make an appointment in our diaries. We'll go into the lounge, shut the door, and say that if the telephone rings we are unavailable. You might feel that is a bit extreme, and you may find it unnecessary to book an appointment. However, if you don't do it this way, make sure that you can communicate with your partner, and them with you, in a way that works properly. Good communication demands time, priority time.

Your Body Talks

You don't always need words to communicate; you constantly use your body. Your posture, the faces you pull, your hand movements, all communicate. A cuddle, a caress, a 'knee squeeze', can all say 'I love you.'

As Heather and I were beginning our courtship I was preaching and she was sitting in the congregation with her mother. Nobody was supposed to have a clue that we were interested in each other. At the end of the meeting the pastor came up and said 'What is going on between you and that Martin girl?' Innocently I said, 'What do you mean?' He said, 'Well, it's obvious. You kept on looking at each other while you were preaching.' Although we had not spoken a word to each other, we were communicating and it was noticed!

Confrontation

Confrontation is a very important part of true communication between husbands and wives. Most of us try to run away from it at times but it is very necessary for maintaining a healthy relationship. When confronting, always confront the issue and never confront the person. Confrontation should always deal with issues, not those who are involved. As a couple we must learn to separate ourselves from the issue before addressing it. Let me give you an example of poor confrontation:

'The telephone bill is huge this quarter. You have been making phone calls that you haven't told me about. It's your fault, it must be you, nobody else could have done it.'

It would be better to say, 'Darling, the phone bill is a lot higher than normal. Can we sit together and look at it? How has it got like this?'

Confrontation should never be a personal attack on each other. Don't avoid it either. 'Sweeping things under the carpet' has never solved anything. In most marriages so much has been swept under the carpet that it is touching the ceiling! Issues do not go away, time is not 'a great healer'. Everything that is ignored and swept under the carpet will have an affect on your life now, and in the future if not dealt with. As a couple you need to commit yourselves to deal with every issue as it arises. At the first opportunity confront the issue and deal with it.

The Guilty Party

Most of us avoid confrontation because we do not handle guilt at all well. In a situation where issues are confronted, don't allow the words you use to make the other person feel guilty. Guilt and condemnation will cause damage if allowed into a marriage. Your goal in confronting an issue should be to resolve the situation, never to leave the other person 'on the floor'.

What causes guilt? One reason is that we don't respond

properly. I had a situation where someone constantly made me feel guilty because their expectations of me were beyond my ability. They were constantly confronting me over issues that I could do little about. Heather saw what was happening and helped me deal with the situation. From that moment I felt as if I had been born again, again. If anything makes you feel guilty except sin that you have committed, then there is something wrong. Even when sin makes you guilty, you should not stay like that because you can repent, confess and be cleansed by the blood of Jesus.

Making it Work

A friend of mine once said, 'Communication is usually impossible but always a miracle.' Unless you are very unusual, the truth is that it is very rare that we achieve full communication with each other. Many people avoid this level of genuine communication. Why? Because it requires you not only to listen but also to open your life. If you are prepared to work through the points I have raised in this chapter, your marriage and your family will receive a real boost.

My Covenant Love

My covenant love to you makes me want to accept you,
Makes me want to lay down my life to serve you.
I want to feel how you feel,
To share your laughter, your times of success,
The times when you feel on top of the world,
And full of confidence.

I want to share the times of heartache too,
To feel the pain of disappointment,
Of your hurts and grief, to weep with you,
And feel the burden of your heart.

How often I want to assure and encourage you,
Yet I want to ask for your forgiveness
Which I frequently fail to do.
At times I'm so unobservant and unthankful
Of the things you have so thoughtfully done;
I treat with ignorant contempt the beauty you created
In the home and, even worse,
Take for granted your expressions of love.

It is sometimes only when I'm away I realise
How precious your tender love actually is to me.
I start to perceive the sacrificial detail you give
To our relationship and I long to take you in my arms
And make up for all the times I neglected to express
My thanks and appreciation.

I simply want to say 'sorry' however inadequately
That communicates my heart to you.
But I want to go forward to live out
My covenant love with you.
I want to communicate how much you mean to me,
That you are the girl of my dreams,
The flower of unique fragrance and beauty
In the garden of my life,
Whose scent satisfies the very core of my being
And causes my heart to beat faster.

I give myself to you afresh,
I surrender my love, my affection, my future, my ambitions,
To our relationship and your success
Within the security of our mutual covenant love,

                                        (Used with permission)

Written by a husband to his wife at the end of one of our
Married Couples Weekends.

Chapter 5

No Entry

It does not matter how long a couple have known each other before they get married; until they begin to live and share their lives together they are really still strangers. It is also possible to live together, and even raise children, and yet remain two isolated individuals. I have met some couples who have been together for thirty or forty years, but know very little about their partner. If that describes you, be encouraged. It is not too late; you can still build a deep relationship and become good friends. God's plan is that every couple should thoroughly enjoy each other's company and long to do things together. Retirement will then be something to look forward to, because you have already learned to spend time together. The alternative is that when the children leave home, two elderly people will find themselves living in the same house, as strangers.

Loneliness is the evidence of a lack of a deep relationship with anyone. It is probably the most painful, hurtful thing a person can ever suffer. Being lonely is avoidable. You do not have to be alone, if you choose to change. If you are willing to open your heart and make sure you have no secrets, no 'no-go' areas from each other, you need never experience that isolation.

As we mentioned in the previous chapter, for the first ten years of our marriage, Heather and I were both afraid that if either of us mentioned certain subjects the other would react badly. Both of us developed the skill of avoiding those topics, which produced 'no-go' areas in our relationship. Neither of us realised that the fears were caused by hurts and rejections we had allowed to take root in our lives. They caused a bondage that made us react badly, and constantly look for acceptance. The more acceptance we got, the more we needed it. Why was that so?

Rejection, and the bondage it brings, is not satisfied by acceptance, no matter how much is given. Freedom will come when the rejection is dealt with, and the bondage broken. Praise God because now we both know that we are *'accepted in the Beloved'* and it is this love that has set us free to love each other. As we drove to Penzance that night we found the strength to begin to be honest. It was one of the greatest moments of our marriage, but it took a long time to get to; I regret the delay now.

We need to allow our partner to have access into our innermost secrets and thoughts; they must get to know who we really are because nobody wants to relate to an external veneer. A veneer simply covers up the real thing. We need to learn to talk honestly.

A Part Truth

How often do you say things that hide the truth? So often we share only the 'successes' in our lives and hide the things we regard as failure. Pride makes us build up a 'total success' image for our partner. God warns us that

> *'Pride goes before destruction, a haughty spirit before a fall,'*   (Proverbs 16:18)

and

> *'Pride only breeds quarrels . . . '*   (Proverbs 13:10)

Where there is contention in a relationship, it isn't hard to find pride at the root.

My mother-in-law once said to me 'Don, we can never win with you, because you are always willing to be wrong.' If we are going to be honest with one another we need to develop this attitude. The Lord is the only one who is always right. The attitude that says, 'I'm right, you are wrong' will ruin a relationship. Another manifestation of the same attitude is, 'It's always me that is wrong.' As those words are spoken, the thought that accompanies them is 'I know I am right.' Stubbornness is sin, and a great hindrance to building relationships.

We need to talk openly about our fears, our desires and the problems we face, share the things that hurt inside. I need to know the things that really hurt Heather and she needs to know what hurts me. So often it seems easier to settle for 'peace at any cost'. That is false peace and never lasts. It is like sitting on the edge of a volcano that is about to erupt. Commit yourselves, long before arguments or problems arise, that you will *'speak the truth in love.'* For,

> *'Do two walk together unless they have agreed to do so?'*
> (Amos 3: 3)

I used to frustrate Heather by hiding from her how I really felt when I was unwell. For me, it was almost a sin to acknowledge anything negative; I felt unable to tell her when I was feeling down. Actually, I thought that this 'super spiritual' reaction was godly! It became so ingrained into my lifestyle, that Heather had to get my friend Mike Darwood, to help her get me to see this. The truth was, I was keeping her out of my life. It was such a relief when I could share things honestly, so that we could stand together. The devil did not stand a chance! It also brought a new depth into our love for each other, for

> *'though one may be overpowered, two can defend themselves. A cord of three strands is not quickly broken.'*
> (Ecclesiastes 4:12)

Ouch!

Some couples discover that as one of them tries to be open, the other reacts wrongly. This stops important issues being faced and worked through. Someone aptly described this as the 'Pain Barrier'. We all need to get to the place where we are committed to going through that barrier. If not, we will never know victory in that area. You may have tried several times, but it seems impossible – don't give up! Find another Christian couple whom you can trust, talk about the difficulty, pray together, they will be pleased to help you.

Past hurts and rejections stop people communicating. Some people react in the heat of a moment with statements like 'You're hopeless!' or 'I wish I'd never married you!' These are like weeds sown into a person's heart and can do untold damage long after they were said. 'Sticks and stones may break my bones, but names will never hurt me' is a lie; words do hurt. Time does not heal; it merely buries the issue. The problem is still there in the subconscious and the 'fruit' produced can't be hidden.

It is not possible to build a strong, deep relationship with someone who is hurt, unless you are prepared to recognize that hurt and do something about it. Together, you can seek the Lord's healing, in an atmosphere of genuine, open love and forgiveness.

Our Problems

If we really believe that we are one, we will see that any problem our partner may have is not 'his' or 'her' problem but 'our' problem. Until we are right on this point, we will confront the person, not the issue, and little will change. It does not matter so much who the issue concerns, we are 'one' and should face the issue together. It is against us! This can make us more vulnerable, as it may have been our actions that caused our partner's bad response in the first place. Be quick to apologize and to ask forgiveness.

It is not our job to change our partner. We must accept

them as they are, in the same way that Christ accepted us. Have you ever seriously considered what you were like when Christ accepted you? I was thoroughly rotten. God says, 'Now accept one another.' Husbands, accept your wives; wives accept your husbands. You will find that in the very act of true acceptance, you will find strength to begin to deal with the faults and weaknesses. When this attitude is right, we can soberly confront any issues, but, choose the moment wisely. The time to do it is not in the middle of an issue, but later at an unemotional moment.

There is often a temptation to express hurt or anger with accusations, shouting or hard words. These don't achieve anything; the Bible tells us that

> '*A gentle answer turns away wrath, but a harsh word stirs up anger.*' (Proverbs 15:1)

Never confront your partner in an aggressive way; always confront the issue. Even when talking about intimate issues don't make it a personal charge. 'You never...' or 'You always...' is an attack. The usual response is for the accused to go on the defensive or throw back an equally hard rebuttal. An accusation seldom brings a satisfactory result. It will only increase the hostility. If you have to face an issue, think about the words you say and be careful to control your volume.

A better approach than 'You never...' is to say 'When you ... I feel...' For example, 'I feel left out and ignored. I may be wrong, but that is how I feel'. This communicates far more than, 'You always ignore me.' When Heather comes to me with a sincere expression of her feelings, I don't have to feel threatened. I am prompted to respond sensitively and discuss the matter in a constructive way.

Relationships – Never on the Line

We need to know that our partner loves us enough not to reject us. Heather and I are secure in this love. I know that whatever she discovers about me, she will not reject me. She also knows that whatever I found out about her, I would not reject her. Our relationship is never on the line. Therefore, we can honestly face issues, knowing that they will never part us. We have committed ourselves to work out any problems we may face.

This level of security and trust does not just happen, it takes time to establish. There is one thing that often damages this trust, which can be avoided with a simple decision and commitment. We have met many couples who have been left with a deep mistrust and insecurity from one act. They have been arguing with each other, and in the emotion of the moment one partner has stormed out, saying 'That's it, I'm leaving.' Often all that happens is that a walk or drive and a period of calming down does enable both partners to think and talk again. However, that statement 'I'm leaving,' will have sown a pernicious weed of doubt that needs removing. Never say those words, however emotional you feel. If you have said them in the past, repent and ask your partner for forgiveness.

If you get involved in a disagreement it may be wise to break off for a short time. Go for a walk alone, or do something in another part of the house. That space will enable you to calm your thoughts, pray and draw on the grace of God. Then **go back** and settle the issue.

When you decide nothing will separate you and that you will never leave each other, a foundation is laid that allows trust to develop. In the early days of a marriage, very few couples really know this security. It comes out of building your life together and it is strengthened as your love is tested. Couples need to express and confess their loyalty for each other. If you have ever been guilty of threatening to leave when things were not going your way, stop playing that childish game. Make a commitment to your partner now, that from today your relationship will never again be on the line. Commit yourself to be loyal to each other at all times.

A Terrible Mistake?

Some Christians live in fear that they have married the wrong partner. The devil loves to encourage that thinking. The truth is that when our marriage is consummated, we are one. The Lord's will is for us to stay one. So, you can face any issue knowing that your relationship is not at stake. As far as God is concerned, there is no such thing as incompatibility. God has given us His grace to work out our relationships.

What's That You Said?

Almost every marriage problem has a root in bad communication. We can be so vague and superficial, but we need to 'tell it like it is'. Communication is crucial to the success of a relationship. Yet it is a skill few of us have learnt to use well.

So, learn to react positively when your partner asks what you would like to do. 'I don't mind. I will do whatever you want to do' is usually a cop out and makes no contribution to the relationship. Be real and say what is in your heart; of course you can add 'If there is something you would rather do, I would be happy for that.' I want Heather to know what my desires for her are and I want to know her desires for me.

Discover the things that motivate your partner. What makes them angry or happy or inspires them? What are their likes and dislikes? One practical result of finding out these things from Heather, is that my washing goes into a basket rather than a pile on the floor!

To help overcome the shyness of sharing these issues, I recommend the following exercise:

Write each other an honest and frank letter. In it include these seven points:
1. What do you like most about your partner?
2. What do you dislike most?

3. Share something with your partner that you have never shared before.
4. Say something about your sexual relationship.
5. Say something about the fun side of your marriage.
6. Say something about the devotional side of your marriage.
7. Share an ambition or desire that is still to be fulfilled in your marriage.

The letters should be written simultaneously and then exchanged. Don't read your partner's letter and write yours in response.

We have used this exercise in marriage seminars all over the world and it has been very effective. Often wives have testified that it was the first letter they had received from their husbands for many, many years.

There have been occasions when serious, deep secrets have been discovered through these letters. Without exception, the result has been growth in the couple's relationship. Before it was confessed, the fear was that the sin would destroy the marriage; the truth is that God works by bringing His light into your darkness. Satan loves darkness and keeping things hidden; it gives him room to work. 1 John 1:7 reads

> *'But if we walk in the light, as He is in the light, we have fellowship with one another, and the blood of Jesus, his Son, purifies us from all sin.'*

If your letters do uncover a secret of this nature, keep things in the light; get pastoral help if it is an issue that you can't resolve between yourselves.

I suggest that you write each other a letter as soon as possible. If your partner has not been reading this book with you, ask them to read this chapter and then encourage them to write a letter to you. It could revolutionise your marriage!

Chapter 6

Love and Forgiveness

'And when you stand praying, if you hold anything against anyone, forgive him, so that your Father in heaven may forgive you your sins.'   (Mark 11:25–26)

Several years ago I was conducting a mission in Northamptonshire. At the end of the series of meetings we had an 'Any Questions' session. On the panel answering the questions were three of us from my team and the local Anglican vicar. During the crusade the vicar had not agreed with everything that we had done but he joined us for this session. Someone stood up and said 'Mr Double has preached this week that if you want to go to heaven, all you have to do is to confess that you are a sinner. He said you must repent of your sin, put your trust in the Lord Jesus Christ, and get washed in the blood of Jesus. Is this right?' With three evangelists on the platform, I expect you can guess what sort of answer we gave! Then it was the vicar's turn to answer and I wondered what he would say. His reply was very profound.

He said, 'I agree with everything my colleagues have just said, but there is one thing that they have left out. Jesus said "If you don't forgive, you will not be forgiven." If you do everything Mr Double has said and don't forgive others, you will go to hell and never make it to heaven.' His statement made quite an impact on me, re-emphasising how serious it is to hold grudges against anyone.

For many people, their lives are a constant round of problems, the root of which is resentment. Often, a deeply held hurt or grudge against someone is at the root of depression. I regularly meet people who come seeking prayer for depression; they appear to get a measure of victory, but do not understand why their problems come back again. The truth is you cannot build a bypass around resentment and hope that the unforgiveness will go away. It must be confronted and then dealt with.

The Greatest Love Words

'I forgive you,' are the greatest love words that can ever be spoken. They are stronger words than 'I love you.' Forgiveness is the cement that keeps the family together. Picture the Lord dying on the cross, His back in shreds, bleeding where He had been whipped. Nails through His hands and feet, a crown of thorns on His head; His face is raw where they have plucked out His beard, people are mocking Him as the soldiers offer Him vinegar to drink. Yet He prays:

> *'Father, forgive them, for they do not know what they are doing.'* (Luke 23:24)

Those are the greatest words of love that have ever been spoken in the universe. Love is far more than what I call the 'sloppy, sentimental slush' that we see and hear so much on the TV. Consider the impact of Jesus' words on the men who had hammered in those nails and plucked out his beard, and on those people who stood around laughing. They heard Him say *'Father, forgive.'*

We cannot love this way in our own strength. However, the Bible tells us that

> *'God has poured out his love into our hearts by the Holy Spirit, whom he has given us.'* (Romans 5:5)

God's love is given to us so that we can forgive as He forgave, and so that we can obey Jesus' command to love our enemies (Matthew 5:44).

Jesus did not say that we will never have enemies; only that when we do, we are to love them. As a preacher once put it, we are to 'love them to death,' to love them until they no longer exist as an enemy. *'Love never fails'* (1 Corinthians 13:8). It is a wonderful thing to be able to love those who deliberately set out to hurt us and truly forgive them.

Soon after I became a Christian, I went through an experience in which I was cruelly used. Then I found myself in a position where I could have committed murder, according to the law, and would have got away with it. At that moment, God filled my heart with His love and grace. I walked over to the person who had misused me and put my arms around him, and said, 'I love you.' I do not know what that did for him, but it did something for me. I could have worked up a huge amount of hatred and resentment, which would have, apart from anything else, severely affected my health in later years. God enabled me to forgive.

It is no good blaming the people you resent, even if it is entirely their fault. You still must forgive them and love them. It is your responsibility before God to forgive.

> *'If your enemy is hungry, feed him; if he is thirsty, give him something to drink. In doing this, you will heap burning coals on his head.'* (Romans 12:20)

We are to bless those who curse us and be good to those who spitefully use us. God never tells us to do anything that we are not able to do and for which He will not give us the grace to carry through.

How Many Times?

The apostle Peter once asked Jesus,

> ' "*Lord how many times shall I forgive my brother when he sins against me? Up to seven times?" Jesus answered, "I tell you, not seven times, but seventy-seven times." *'
>
> (Matthew 18:21–22)

Some translations say seventy times seven, but Jesus was not saying only forgive four hundred and ninety times. If you do forgive someone that often, by the time you get to Time 491, it will be so natural to forgive that you will just go on forgiving! Peter could testify to the Lord's repeated forgiveness. He had many failures, yet on the day of Pentecost he was the man God so greatly used.

Receiving Forgiveness

Many people find it hard to receive forgiveness. They sin against another person, who forgives them, but somehow they cannot forgive themselves. They constantly live under condemnation, which saps their spiritual life and sometimes destroys them. We need to see that it is an issue of pride if you cannot forgive yourself. The Bible says,

> '*God opposes the proud but gives grace to the humble.*'
>
> (James 4:6)

Accept the grace of God and His forgiveness.

Paul expressed a wonderful attitude when he said to the Church at Corinth,

> '*If you forgive anyone, I also forgive him. And what I have forgiven – if there was anything to forgive – I have forgiven in the sight of Christ for your sake.*'
>
> (2 Corinthians 2:10)

Periodically I get letters from people who say, 'Will you forgive me?' Most are people I have never met or known that they had done anything wrong. However, they are people who want to be right and have the right attitude.

You will never grow in God until this issue of forgiveness is right in your life. Before Paul knew they needed forgiveness he had forgiven them. Paul was concerned about keeping himself clean and right before God.

Many people live with 'a chip on their shoulder'. Sometimes it is because they feel that their parents have failed them. Others are orphans and feel that life has dealt them a cruel blow. Deep down inside, if the secrets of their hearts were revealed, the reality is that they blame God for it. Others may have a hang-up because they are illegitimate.

It is wonderful to realise that Jesus knows exactly how you feel; He can identify with you. But even better, He can bring you to the place where you can be freed. Have you ever considered the life of Jesus? He was born of the Virgin Mary, the Holy Spirit being His Father, yet Joseph accepted Him as his own son. As a result, Jesus was accused of being illegitimate. What is more, both Joseph and Mary had illegitimacy in their lineage, according to the genealogies recorded in Matthew 1 and Luke 3.

Jesus can identify with you and wants to heal your hurt, so that you can forgive and forget. Let me explain what I mean about forgetting. If you forgive someone for something they did, it doesn't mean you will never think of it again. Their action can come back to your remembrance because we have not been promised freedom from temptation. Forgetting means you won't dwell on that thought or allow it any room in your life.

Let me illustrate this: Phil and Paul had a gossip session about me. Phil, later, was in the presence of the Lord and got convicted about it. He now comes to me and says 'Don, I have been saying horrible things and gossiping about you. I am really sorry. I want you to forgive me.' I reply 'Yes Phil, I forgive you.' Having got right he goes on his way, and I have really forgiven him. Two days later, the devil whispers in my ear, 'You can't really trust Phil again. He goes around gossiping about you. Go and ask Paul if he has said anything else.' What do you do with thoughts like that? If you harbour them, you have not forgiven; if you reject them, you have forgiven. That is the difference. It doesn't mean that the thought will not come back and try to invade your life again; it does mean that you won't allow your mind to think about it. You have to say, 'No I am having nothing to do with it.'

Forgiveness – Key to a Healthy Life

Forgiveness is a key to health. So much disease comes from the basic root of unforgiveness. It is a fact that one form of arthritis is caused from bitterness and resentment. However, far more damage is done on the spiritual side of life through resentment.

We need to learn to forgive the people who do not agree with us. Do you forgive the local church that does not hold the same doctrines as you? Are there people in your own church whom you need to forgive? In some churches I have met people who have not spoken to other members of the same church for more than twenty years. Is it surprising that those churches are almost empty? The Bible says,

> *'If anyone says, "I love God," yet hates his brother, he is a liar. For anyone who does not love his brother, whom he has seen, cannot love God, whom he has not seen.'*
>
> (1 John 4:20)

To say that you are right with God when you are not right with your mother, father, husband, wife, church leader or anyone else is a contradiction.

Sadly many homes are split by unforgiveness. For instance, when young people become Christians and their parents are not saved, it can lead to all kinds of tensions in the home. If you know young people in this situation help them to live a life of forgiveness, love and service. Their parents will never be won by conflict, arguments and fights.

The Family – a Perfect Opportunity

In the family there will be plenty of opportunities to forgive. Husbands, as head of your family, it is your responsibility to start forgiveness, even if your wife is 100 per cent at fault (which is very unlikely). We are to love our wives as Christ loved the Church, when He gave himself for it (Ephesians 5:25). On the cross, Jesus was totally right and humanity was totally wrong, yet the Lord initiated forgiveness.

Do not allow long periods to pass without forgiving. Take a lead in asking for forgiveness as well. It might be painful, but it takes the sting out of the situation and keeps love flowing. So get in quickly! To try to hold out for as long as possible is the result of pride and is a recipe for disaster. Bed is not the place for reconciliation. If there is a problem, deal with it that day.

> *'In your anger do not sin: Do not let the sun go down while you are still angry.'*   (Ephesians 4:26)

Where necessary, take a lead in apologizing and ask for forgiveness. After many years of practice it is still difficult for me at times, but I know there is no other way if you want a successful marriage.

A basic human problem is our tendency to avoid taking responsibility for our actions. The first person who ever did this was Adam, when he said to God *'The woman you put here with me . . . '* (Genesis 3:12). He was really saying, 'It is her fault, not mine.' Also, Adam was implying that he thought God was wrong to give her to him in the first place. We must learn to be responsible for the things we do and say. The longer we hold out, the more tension grows. Remember, it is a lot easier to move a mole hill than it is to move a mountain!

Where love is really alive, there must be forgiveness constantly flowing. I have met some couples who have had problems over thirty years and not forgiven each other. I believe that to delay even an hour is too long! Asking for forgiveness takes the sting out of the situation and keeps love flowing. Husbands, wives, parents, children and in-laws need lots of forgiving. The closer you are to people the easier it is for them to hurt you!

It Works!

We need to be known as forgiving people. Young people, get into the habit of forgiving now and maintain a spirit of forgiveness all the way through your life; then you will be truly blessed. Teach your children from the youngest age to ask for forgiveness and to apologize. This is a vital part in training and shaping their lives. Then, when they eventually marry and have a family of their own, this attitude will be a natural part of their lives.

If I know you are a forgiving person, I will have no fear of coming to you. It means you love me and perfect love casts out all fear (1 John 4:18). If I think you will be hard and callous towards me, I will never come to you and share anything. It is vital in our families that forgiveness is freely flowing. It is another key to keeping our relationships fresh.

Once when I was sharing these things in an early morning men's meeting I concluded by saying, 'Go home, put your arms around your wife and tell her that you love her. Then ask her to forgive you for all the things that you have ever done wrong.'

That evening we had a big rally with hundreds of people present. At the end of the service, a lady came up to me and very directly said, 'Mr Double, what did you do to my husband this morning?' I said, 'I do not know, you tell me,' to which she replied, 'He came home and put his arms around me and told me that he loved me! Do you know what he did next? He asked me to forgive him for all the things that he had ever done wrong. He has never done that before, and it is wonderful!' That evening they took me out for a meal to celebrate!

I want to finish by giving you four steps to forgiveness.

1. Forgiveness is an act of your will

It is no good saying that you are too hurt to forgive. No-one has ever been put under so much pressure that they could not forgive. God has given you a free will. No-one can ever take that from you. By an act of your will you have to say 'I want to forgive.' If you have no other reason to do so, that God has said it in His word should be reason enough.

2. Receive the ability to forgive

Having come to the place where you say, 'I want to forgive,' you must receive the ability to do it. Open your heart and mind to God and pray 'Lord, please fill me with your love.'

3. Speak out forgiveness

I don't believe in a general, meaningless 'sorry'. We need forgiveness with 'backbone'. It has to have some strength in it, some meaning; eyeball to eyeball forgiveness is specific – 'Dad, I forgive you' or 'Mum, I forgive you.'

Even if it is not possible to say the words face to face, it is still vital that the words pass your lips. Sometimes it is a battle, and by an act of the will we have to make ourselves say the words, but it does work.

4. Forgive, then forget

The way you can tell whether you have forgiven or not, is if when you recall a specific event you know that it has no effect on you.

As you have been reading this chapter, God may have put His finger on some areas of your life where you need to forgive. Perhaps He has spoken to you about unresolved issues between you and your spouse. That is great because it shows that God really does care for you and wants you to be completely whole. So, if there is something that needs to be put right, would you now reread these four points on how to forgive.

71

Now we need to talk to Father. Please put the person's name into the blanks.

> 'Heavenly Father, thank you for the love you have
> for me. Thank you that it is consistent and never fails
> and you are always wanting the very best for me.
> Thank you for showing me this area of my life where
> I have been unforgiving. Lord, please give me the
> ability to forgive (name) ....
> I receive your love to do that, right now.'

Now speak out that forgiveness (if you can do that face to face with the person please do so):

> '(Name) .... I forgive you for .... '

Chapter 7

Covenants and Vows

The word 'covenant' is not used very often these days, but I hope to show you, in this chapter, the relevance and value of making a covenant. In Genesis chapter 9 we read about God making the first covenant.

> *'Then God said to Noah and to his sons with him: "I now establish my covenant with you and with your descendants after you ... I establish my covenant with you: Never again will all life be cut off by the waters of a flood; never again will there be flood to destroy the earth."'* (Genesis 9:8–9, 11)

God made an everlasting commitment to mankind and the whole of creation, and confirmed it with a sign that we can still see today.

> *'I have set my rainbow in the clouds, and it will be the sign of the covenant between me and the earth.'* (Genesis 9:13)

Every time I see a rainbow, my first reaction is, 'Lord, thank you that you are a covenant keeping God.' He does not break His word and the rainbow proves it. When you see a rainbow, remember that God keeps covenant and what He has said He will do, is what He will do. This is the only covenant in the Bible that has an ending specified (Genesis 8:22) – all the other covenants that God made are eternal.

The next covenant we read of is in Genesis 15 & 17. As you read the details of this covenant you will find that it is different from the covenant God made with Noah. How? In the Noahic covenant man did nothing. God initiated it and committed Himself to it. For Abraham it was different, he had to do something for this covenant to be effective. Abraham had to make a sign in his own body of the covenant that God made with him. That sign was circumcision, the removal of his foreskin.

The first covenant, with Noah, was made totally from God's side. It did not depend on man meeting any conditions. But, for the Abrahamic covenant to be valid, Abraham and his descendants had to do something.

> *'Whether born in your household or bought with your money, they must be circumcised. My covenant in your flesh is to be an everlasting covenant. Any uncircumcised male, who has not been circumcised in the flesh, will be cut off from his people; he has broken my covenant.'*
>
> (Genesis 17:13–14)

The covenant that God made with Abraham is still applicable, although the condition has changed. For us, the New Testament makes it clear that our hearts are 'circumcised' through water baptism. There is much I could say about this, but I would recommend that you read Romans, chapters four to six.

Scarred for Life

In many cultures today, making a covenant is still a very important part of life, or to describe it more accurately, people still 'cut covenant'. Usually, the people making a covenant will cut their wrists, then mingle their blood with wine or water, and then drink it. Sometimes they will rub dirt into the wound on the wrist, so that it scars and there is a permanent mark of the covenant they have made. It becomes a reminder for them, and a sign to others, that this person is 'in covenant'.

Why is that significant? If you see a covenant scar, you become aware that there is more to this person than meets the eye. It means that if you are in a dispute or argument and see the sign of covenant you need to be careful. The individual you are dealing with is not alone, he has a 'brother' who is committed to him. He may be stronger, or more powerful, or have greater influence than you, so be wary. When a covenant is cut, part of the agreement that is made is 'what I have belongs to you. If you are in difficulty I will do everything I can to help you.' As you consider your relationship with God, be aware that the covenant you share entitles you to the same protection. There is more to us than meets the eye! God is 'backing' us.

There are several other instances of people cutting covenant in the Old Testament. Often they had to kill a lamb and cut it in two, then the people making the covenant did something unusual. They would walk between the two parts of the carcass, in a figure of eight. That shape is called the 'eternal figure' because it is a continuous line and it symbolised the duration of the covenant.

Biblical covenants were always marked by a sacrifice. This is a powerful image for us, because to enter a permanent relationship with God requires two things: a covenant and a sacrifice. The covenant represents a final irrevocable commitment. Once you have entered a covenant there is no way out as far as God is concerned. A sacrifice symbolises the death of each party to that covenant.

> *'In the case of a will* [covenant], *it is necessary to prove the death of the one who made it, because a will* [covenant] *is in force only when somebody has died; it never takes effect while the one who made it is living.'*
>
> (Hebrews 9:16–17)

When they cut the lamb in half, symbolically it said 'I lay my life down for you.'

The sacrifice represents me; it dies in my place. As I enter the covenant I enter through death. That is significant because I have no more right to live for myself, I live for my covenant partner. It is impossible to be in covenant and to live independently. A covenant instructs the agreement of an irrevocable two-way commitment.

Tied to Each Other

> *'The Lord is acting as the witness between you and the wife of your youth, because you have broken faith with her, though she is your partner, the wife of your marriage covenant.'* (Malachi 2:14)

Understand that by the time Malachi lived, Israel had come to view marriage as a relationship for which they could set their own standards. They no longer were living under the commandments that God had given to Moses, but had started to go their own way. Instead of following God's plan, Israel had begun to copy the customs of the nations that lived around them. As a result they were putting their own conditions on marriage, and were cancelling it on their own terms. Through Malachi, God reminds them, and us, that He views marriage differently. It is a covenant. Just like other covenants, marriage involves two parties – husband and wife. In the same way that blood was involved in the Abrahamic covenant, so with marriage. Usually on the first occasion of intercourse for a virgin wife, her hymen is broken and blood is shed. Then there is the sign of the covenant – a rainbow for Noah and circumcision for Abraham. For us in the western world the wedding ring is our sign of covenant.

I believe that the secret of a successful marriage is to understand the covenant you have made. As you see the significance of what I have written and then apply it to your life you will have a very firm foundation to build on.

In Genesis 1 and 2 we read of the act of Creation and how God made Adam and Eve. Note that it was not Adam's decision to have a mate. It was God's decision, man had nothing to do with it. Marriage was God's idea and God formed Eve and presented her to Adam. God established the terms of the covenant relationship in which He united them. They should be one flesh, a union; I like to use the word 'merger', instead of 'partnership' to describe the relationship. Think about the business world for a moment. If two companies become partners, they will both continue to have their own identities. However, if they merge then one business disappears and becomes part of a bigger whole. After a time it is impossible to find two separate entities. This is a good illustration of marriage, a merger of two into one. It's not a partnership, as we do not live on an equal basis. I no longer live for myself, but for my husband and vice versa.

From the beginning, the relationship Adam and Eve had was a three-dimensional union: God and Adam, God and Eve, Adam and Eve. We need God in our marriage in the same way. Our relationship must be 'vertical' and 'horizontal.' In Ecclesiates 4:9–12 there is a beautiful illustration of this 3-D relationship:

> *'Two are better than one, because they have a good return for their work: If one falls down, his friend can help him up. But pity the man who falls and has no one to help him up! Also, if two lie down together, they will keep warm. But how can one keep warm alone? Though one may be overpowered, two can defend themselves. A cord of three strands is not quickly broken.'*
>
> (Ecclesiastes 4:9–12)

'Two are better than one, because they have good return for their work' (verse 9). Everything that God does is done with purpose and He does it well. He has told us why He made Eve:

77

> *'The LORD God said, "It is not good for the man to be alone. I will make a helper suitable for him."'*
>
> (Genesis 2:18)

Adam, as all men do, needed to share his life with someone.

'If one falls down, his friend can help him up. But pity the man who falls and has no one to help him up!' (verse 10). Don and I have proved the truth of this often in our marriage. On occasions when I have been 'down', he has been strong and has lifted me up. When he has been down, I have done the same for him. When two become one they are 'in it' together, and their aim should be to help each other, not living for their own benefit.

'Also, if two lie down together, they will keep warm. But how can one keep warm alone?' (verse 11). God is so practical. Companionship is a wonderful blessing, physically as much as in any other part of our lives.

'Though one may be overpowered, two can defend themselves. A cord of three strands is not quickly broken' (verse 12). Some time ago we refitted our kitchen. To finish off the decoration, I wanted to get a rope to go around the room, between the ceiling and the wall. I had to search hard for the right type of rope, because most are now made from synthetic materials, and I wanted a 'natural' one made of hemp. Finally I went to a Ships' Chandler in a sea-port near to our home. He said he could supply what I wanted but would have to make it for me. He told me that hemp ropes are only made from three cords because that gives the strongest rope; ropes made from four, five, or more strands get progressively weaker. That amazed me, wisdom recorded three thousand years ago in the Bible was still being used and was reliable. What is the threefold cord that Ecclesiastes refers to? You, your partner and God; when God comes in to make the threefold cord in our marriage. The 'Maker's Instructions' do make sense and we will do well to take heed of them.

When a covenant was cut in Old Testament times, various items were exchanged in the ritual, which often included items of clothing (see the covenant David and Jonathan made, 1 Samuel 18:1–4). The exchange expressed what had been agreed and, although it may not be recognized, we still do the same today. In Britain we have a recognized symbol of the marriage covenant – the wedding ring. My ring communicates to every one that I meet, that I am in covenant with my husband. The ring also signifies that everything I am belongs to Don, and that everything that he is belongs to me. The wedding ceremony is not just something that is 'done', or a social event. It marks the commencement of a covenant that is not to be treated lightly. I think it is because we have lost the understanding of the covenant in the wedding ceremony that so many people find it easy to get divorced.

Getting on with Each Other

God's intention was that a man and woman should live together in harmony, within a marriage covenant. The divorce courts today are full of people saying they want their marriage to end because they are 'incompatible'. I do not believe that for a Christian this is an option. My reason is that God has given us His grace to help us relate to each other. It is a rewarding study to look at the references to 'grace' in the New Testament, and one I would recommend to you. As you do it, you'll find that almost every time the gift of grace is referred to, the context is to do with relationships.

Don and I have found that in our marriage God's grace is essential. Sometimes we get into disagreement and if we chose we could argue for hours. However, the moment we bring God into the situation it changes. We have learnt (sometimes painfully), that the first thing we should do when we have a disagreement, is to turn to God. That is the joy of having the 'third cord' in our marriage and it gives us real strength.

Forgotten Vows?

Once you have been married for a while, it is easy to forget what you did commit yourselves to, and exactly what you did say when you got married. I want to make this teaching on covenants very practical by now looking at those vows you made. Can you remember them? Although the words you said may be different (and these are the man's vows), what follows is the basic commitment every married person makes:

> I will take this woman to be my wife, to live with her according to the law of God. I promise to love her, comfort her, honour and keep her; and forsaking all others, I will remain faithful to her alone, while we both are alive.
> I call upon the persons here present to witness that I take this woman to be my wife, to have and to hold from this day forward, for better for worse, for richer for poorer, in sickness and in health, to love and to cherish, till death do us part, according to God's holy law and this is my solemn vow.

' . . . for better for worse, for richer for poorer, in sickness and in health . . .' We are committed to an unconditional love. Even when you discover the bad things; when habits irritate, when circumstances are against you, your love should be consistent. Love is a commitment that always has acceptance at its core. You cannot love someone and not accept them. It's impossible to say 'I love you' and refuse to accept them as they are. Christ accepted us just as we were, disfigured by sin, because He loved us. In the same way we must love and accept each other.

Husbands, you promised to comfort your wife. If you said the 'new' vows, you probably said 'love, cherish and worship'; 'honour and comfort' are in the old version. Comfort is something that women need. It includes showing affection, particularly when things go wrong.

Honour is a word that has fallen out of everyday use. It means to 'look up to', 'respect', 'to hold in a place of esteem'. When you got married, you said you would honour your spouse. What does that mean, because it applies to both husbands and wives? At its most basic, to honour means that you will not demean your spouse in front of other people. I think that is the worst thing a wife can ever do to her husband and yet it happens so easily. When you meet friends over a cup of coffee and you start 'women talk', how often does the subject get on to the failings of your men? It may seem that criticism, pulling them down, magnifying their weaknesses, add spice to the conversation, but you must **stop it**. As wives, we should never talk to anyone about our husbands in a derogatory way.

Husbands, 'keep' your wives. Meet her needs, which is more than just giving her enough housekeeping money. God has made you to be the head of your wife. Provide for her spiritually, mentally and emotionally. The new vows use the word 'protect'. Husbands need to protect their wives from emotional pressure. I know that I appreciate Don's care for me most when I am under pressure and he does something to help. At those times, when the pressures of ministry, office and home build up, he takes authority and does something that relieves the pressure.

The Bible says that you should honour your wife *'as the weaker partner'* (1 Peter 3:7). Physically a woman's body is not weaker than a man's body. A woman's body can take much more pain than a man can – ask any woman who has had children! So, how are women weaker? I would suggest that we are weaker emotionally; we are less able to control our emotional responses. It is an area where husbands need to develop sensitivity so they know how their wife is reacting. At times it may take some effort, but do make sure that your wife is not under emotional pressure. If she is, do something to protect her.

The traditional vows had the wife saying she would obey. Modern vows have dropped the word, but the Bible still says the wife is to obey (Titus 2:5) and to submit

(Ephesians 5:22; Colossians 3:18; 1 Peter 3:1). It is there in print, and we avoid those words at our peril. Obedience to our husband is something that some of us find hard. Why? I have found that the most common reason is because you were not taught to as a child. Today the trend is to rebel against authority and so there are few models of obedience for us to follow. Independence and self-reliance are held to be great qualities but in truth are often covers for sin. If you are fighting the command to obey, you are fighting the Word of God, and how ever hard you try you can't change it. If you want your marriage to work, get back to the Bible and do what it says. God requires the wife to obey and submit to her husband.

To be obedient and submissive does not mean I am a doormat. I am a person with ideas and a God-made personality that I need to express. To be obedient does not mean I am a second-class citizen or have a weak character, quite the contrary. I obey my husband because God tells me to, and that is the only reason. Don does not get my obedience because he is incredibly super-spiritual; he has got 'feet of clay' like other men. I obey him because the Word of God tells me to love and obey him and I am determined to live according to God's Word.

When you said your vows, you committed yourself to a covenant. Those words still stand today because it is an irrevocable commitment. There are several phrases to which I have not referred: 'till death us do part', and 'forsaking all others' which literally means turning your back on every other option, for your spouse. You committed yourself to 'be faithful according to God's holy law'. Whether you were a Christian when you got married or not, go back to the Word of God and find out what He says about marriage. Studying this book will help, but it is not a substitute for the Bible itself. God wants your marriage to be a success; if you do too, get into the Word and obey it.

PART TWO

Loving One Another

Chapter 8

Little Things Mean a Lot

'Husbands, love your wives, just as Christ loved the Church and gave himself up for her.' (Ephesians 5:25)

'Husbands ought to love their wives as their own bodies. He who loves his wife loves himself. After all, no-one ever hated his own body, but he feeds and cares for it, just as Christ does the church.' (Ephesians 5:28–29)

Sowing Seeds

Husbands, we are called to love our wives in the same way that Christ loved the Church. This is a high calling, and very different from the picture presented to us by Hollywood and the things that we see on our television screens. It is a fact that TV programmes have a great influence on people; they affect people's mind-sets and sow seeds that produce unrighteous behaviour. Many programmes portray a very poor image of family life. In most major films the hero is immoral, sleeping with the heroine or a new acquaintance. We need to stand strongly against this. There is a spiritual law that applies to every person: they will reap a harvest from what they sow.

What seeds are you sowing in your mind – seeds of immorality and loose morals, or the seed of God's word? God's word is our only defence against the media and the lack of morals in our society. Let us not compare ourselves with how others behave. God has given us a model of how to love our wives in Jesus. He may seem a high example to follow, but we will never get anywhere unless we have a goal. To love your wife like this, you must be willing to lay down your life for her. Is she the most important person in your life? Sadly, I meet too many wives starved of this kind of love.

There is much confusion about what love is. God is love (1 John 4:8), but how do we love? Don Francisco says in one song 'Love is not a feeling, it is an act of your will.' Husbands, is that your understanding or have you been taught from films and TV? There we find love equated to sex and it is often measured by what happens in bed. Sex is important and a wonderful gift from God to married couples. However, love is far more than sex and the sexual act should be the product of a loving relationship. To discover true love a major lesson we need to learn is that little things mean a lot.

Imperfect Vessels

Even if you feel you have a 'difficult' wife, it is good to remember that God loved us when we were unlovely. Your wife may not be the 'perfect woman' you thought she was when you married her, but you should still love her as Christ loves the Church. Even today, Christ loves the Church with all its imperfections. Love has a transforming effect and makes submission easy. As you love your wife, it becomes easier for her to submit to that love and your life together will be more harmonious and happy.

Love is not just an expression of gushy emotions. It is practical. So how does love like this work? When I was a young man there was a popular song called 'Little things mean a lot!' How true that statement is and if we are willing, it can transform our marriage. As we look together at some practical points, honestly consider how you measure up, be open and eager for God to change you.

Tell your wife every day that you love her

I travel a lot in ministry and spend over 50% of my time each year away from my wife. Yet even when I am hundreds of miles away, I will telephone Heather every evening to tell her I love her. If it is impossible to phone, I will write to her every day and make sure that I include telling her that I love her. Wives need to hear this from us. Don't just take it for granted that she knows. It is important to reassure her of your love for her. If you are a husband that finds it difficult to express your love, be encouraged – the more you say 'I love you', the easier it becomes.

Show by your actions that you love your wife

Little things do mean a lot. It is not enough to show affection on special days such as wedding anniversaries and birthdays. When things have gone wrong in a marriage, I usually find that it is not the big things, but the little things that have been neglected. No woman can hold out long against a man who takes note of the little things. By 'little things' I mean buying your wife flowers from time to time, or sending a card; in some way making an effort to express what you feel about her.

On one crusade, I saw a remarkable effect from this teaching on 'little things'. The day after I spoke, the local florist was inundated with business. Eventually the shop manager asked one of his customers, 'What is going on? Why are all these men buying flowers for their wives?' The man told him that the evangelist at the tent crusade had preached this. The florist replied, 'If his preaching has this effect, I should go along myself and see.' And he did!

Other little things can include buying a box of chocolates (if she isn't dieting). To unexpectedly buy a bottle of her favourite perfume is another way of showing how much you care. Every so often take her out for a special dinner or a weekend away. Make it your business to find out the things that please her. Be creative; as you begin to think and pray you will find the ideas are endless. Keep the element of surprise alive in your marriage. It is these 'little things' that help to keep a freshness in your relationship.

Remembering her birthday and your wedding anniversary is very important. I know of one couple who have a celebration meal each month on the anniversary day on which they were married. Sometimes they go to a restaurant, but other times they have a special meal at home by candlelight. As the children have grown up, they have come to accept this as a normal occurrence and gladly let their parents have one evening a month to themselves. It may not be always possible to buy an expensive meal out or even to make a lavish one at home. However a simple meal, lovingly prepared in a romantic setting, can be one of these little things that mean a lot.

If your wife asks you for a dress, take her out and buy her two! The Bible says

> *'If someone asks you for your cloak, give him your coat also. Go the second mile.'*   (Matthew 5:40–42)

The answer of course is to keep your wife well supplied so that she doesn't have to ask! If you feel that you cannot afford it, ask the Lord to provide a miracle for you. He is our true source and His resources are limitless – He can afford it! These things are too important to let them slip by. When was the last time you took your wife out and bought her something new to wear? (And I am not including Christmas or birthday or her asking because she was desperate.)

Seek to be creative. If you become predictable the element of surprise is lost and with it, what you are trying to express. For instance, I often send Heather flowers when I travel overseas and she has come to almost expect them after I have left. Once a bouquet of flowers arrived as usual. Then, on the next day a bunch of carnations was delivered with a note saying how much I loved her. On the next day, much to Heather's surprise a big bouquet of red roses arrived. You don't have to copy what I did but you can be creative and keep that element of surprise alive. The principle that I am trying to communicate is – **be thoughtful**. It is really the little things that count.

Let your wife know that you delight in her

She needs your encouragement and to know constantly that you find pleasure in her. Don't just praise her when you are alone together, but do so in front of others, especially your children. Let them know that they have the best mother in the world; the best gift that you can give your children is parents who really love each other. Never be critical of your wife. Watch what God is doing in her life and encourage her by telling her when you see something good happen.

Heather and I enjoy each other's company. There is no area of my life that I want her excluded from. She is my best friend and I am hers.

Help build her faith

Encourage your wife to use her faith to get answers to her prayers and to believe that God will supply her personal needs. Do not misunderstand me, it is our responsibility to provide for our wives. The Bible is quite blunt:

> '*If anyone does not provide for his relatives, and especially for his immediate family, he has denied the faith and is worse than an unbeliever.*' (1 Timothy 5:8)

However, there may be some things she doesn't **need** which she would like in the home that she could reach out in faith for.

I have found that the children soon catch on with this too. When my son Stephen was about three years old, he wanted some red wellington boots. We told him to pray

and ask Jesus for them, which he did. The next day someone who knew nothing about this, took him out and bought
him a pair of red wellington boots! You can imagine the
impression that made on his young life.

Protect her

> 'Husbands, in the same way be considerate as you live
> with your wives, and treat them with respect as the
> weaker partner and as heirs with you of the gracious gift
> of life, so that nothing will hinder your prayers.'

(1 Peter 3:7)

After travelling around the world, I am convinced that
this does not primarily refer to the wife being the weaker
vessel physically. In some areas of the world, the wife does
all the work. She tills the ground, milks the cows, cares for
the animals, runs the home and bears as many children as it
is possible to produce. She is very likely to work to the
moment of confinement and then almost immediately
resume her work after the birth.

After watching the kind of work women in Africa do for
example, I am convinced that by the 'weaker vessel' Peter is
not referring to physical weakness. I think he is saying
women are weaker emotionally. It is the husband's responsibility to protect his wife by taking pressure off her. This
involves taking financial responsibility from her. I do not
believe that any woman should have the financial worries
of the home. Even if the wife is the bookkeeper, it is still
the husband's responsibility, as head, to see that the
finances are there to pay the bills.

When it is the time of the month for your wife's period, it
is a time when she needs extra care and understanding. I
keep a note in my diary so that I can make special allow-
ances and provide extra care for my wife. If I find her
getting a little tense, I know why. It is not because we have
fallen out, but that she just needs that extra care and understanding. So many husbands are insensitive in this area,
which can cause a build-up of tension until their wife

explodes. By sensitively caring for your wife, you can do a lot to relieve these situations.

Be observant

It is very important to be observant and to let your wife know that you have noticed things. We should watch out for those occasions when our wives go out of their way to please us. For instance, when they have worked really hard in the home or have done something special with the children. Do not take these things for granted but ensure you express your appreciation. These courtesies are often given to friends and visitors, but forgotten at home.

For example, my wife had a new hairstyle some time ago. When she came home, I couldn't honestly say that I liked it, but I did say, 'It is different' (and it was). I did not tell a lie or pretend that I liked it, but I did let her know that I had noticed. When your wife rearranges the home while cleaning it, be observant and encourage her.

Be a good listener

Your wife needs to know that she has access to you and that you are willing to listen to her. Does she know that you will go out of your way to understand her? I am amazed how many men have been married for twenty or thirty years and yet still do not understand their wives. Too many men involved in the ministry will freely give time to counsel and listen to the problems of others and yet won't listen to the problems of their own wives.

> *'The husband does not have authority over his own body, but the wife does.'*   (1 Corinthians 7:4 NKJV)

Your ears are part of your body, let your wife have power over your ears; give time to listen to what she has to say.

Spend time together. Too many marriage problems are caused because church activities are given a higher priority in Christians' lives than their marriage and family life.

Giving time to the family is different from giving time to your wife. I believe you should give your prime time to your wife. Find time to be alone with her and do things together. Changing your priorities in this way may upset your vicar or pastor, particularly if you are involved in some form of leadership, but this is important. Be honest and discuss what is happening to your marriage with your church leaders.

Once when I was counselling a couple, the Lord said to me, 'The problem is that the wife is still looking for a husband.' When I said this, she burst into tears – they had been married for some years. They were two people living under the same roof, sleeping in the same bed, but living independent lives. One goal I set them was to cancel some things in their diary and make sure they made time to spend with each other.

A major cause of marriage problems today is the increasing demand for employees to travel or live away from home for long periods of time. If a marriage is not built strongly before this happens, it will never get built under those conditions. Also, the temptation to have an affair will be high. It is better to seek alternative employment even if this means lowering one's standard of living. Surely it is better to have a happy marriage than a job that puts strain and pressure on your relationship.

> *'Better a meal of vegetables where there is love than a fattened calf with hatred.'*   (Proverbs 15:17)

Only after the relationship is strong might it be right to resume travelling, if this is the call on a person's life.

Be considerate
We need to be good-mannered towards our wives. Open doors and help her with her coat. Make sure she is seated comfortably at the table before sitting yourself. Do not forget to introduce her to others. Make sure that you immediately introduce your wife, and let her feel she really is

wanted whenever she is around. So many wives feel unwanted, just a convenience, as a servant in the home or just there to look after the children.

Make sure that you dress and smell in a way that is attractive to your wife. It is important to me to know how Heather likes me to dress and what deodorants she likes me to wear. I want to please her.

Another practical point is to keep your bedroom tidy. Avoid those things that irritate your wife, so make it your business to find out those things that annoy her. Ask her to be honest and then make sure that you do not do those things again. You will find that it will have a remarkable effect in your marriage.

Make sure that your wife is sexually fulfilled

> *'The wife's body does not belong to her alone but also to her husband. In the same way, the husband's body does not belong to him alone but also to his wife. Do not deprive each other except by mutual consent and for a time, so that you may devote yourselves to prayer. Then come together again so that Satan will not tempt you because of your lack of self-control.'*

> (1 Corinthians 7:4–5)

I find that many marriage problems and all sorts of symptoms stem from problems with sexual relationships. Irritability, bad temper (especially with the wife and children) and an inferiority complex are often symptoms of a poor sexual relationship.

Too many men, when it comes to sexual relationships, are selfish. Our main motive should be to fulfil our wife, to bring her to a climax, not merely to bring ourselves to orgasm. I believe that sexual relationships came under the curse at the Fall, the same as every other part of life. However, it is God's will that every couple should have complete fulfilment in every way, no matter how much you have failed in this area in the past. With the Lord's help, you can get it right and now enjoy a full sexual experience. You can pray about this, because God **is** interested in your sex life and wants it to be fulfilling; after all it was His idea in the first place!

The Act of Marriage by Tim and Beverley LaHaye, is a superb book on this subject. It has been tremendously helpful to couples who have problems in this area.

The best fulfilment in sexual relationships comes from loving each other, all day, from early in the morning. You should not expect your wife just to 'switch on' when you go to bed. Love-making is not just something that happens when you get to bed. It should be the climax of the whole day spent for each other, showing that you are interested in each other's whole person. Make the most of the time you do have together.

We need to realize the emotional differences between a husband and wife. A man can be turned on simply by seeing his wife undress and immediately be ready for intercourse, but a woman is different. She is aroused sexually through the other senses, particularly her sense of touch. We need to discover the things that stimulate our wives. As God has made each woman different, so each woman differs in the way she is aroused.

Husbands, has your love grown cold? Can you remember a time when you loved your wife more than you do now? Then you need to seek God to renew that love in you again. If a man does not love his wife, he cannot love God and if a man cannot treat his wife properly, he will lack reality in his Church life. His worship will be substandard and if he has any sort of ministry it will lack power and effectiveness. When we get our homes right, the Church will become effective in reaching our world. If we get our families right, people will be queuing up at our doors to find out our secret.

I believe that these practical points I have shared will help to transform any marriage in which the couple wants to go for God's best.

94

Ten Commandments for Husbands

1. Love your wife, as Christ loved the Church, laying down your life for her so that she may become mature in Christ (Ephesians 5:25).
2. Be considerate of your wife, for God did not intend her to bear undue emotional pressure (1 Peter 3:7).
3. Never bear grudges. Forgive your wife as God forgave you (Ephesians 4:32 and Colossians 3:13).
4. Lead your wife and family into the paths of righteousness; impart spiritual life and godly fear to them (Ephesians 5:23).
5. Be the head of the family, giving them proper security, love, fatherhood and protection, as God intended (1 Corinthians 11:3).
6. Live joyfully with your wife, remembering that she is God's gift to you (Genesis 2).
7. Bless and praise your wife; tell her that she is the best wife in the world (Proverbs 31:28–29).
8. Believe in your wife in order for her to be the wife God wants you to have. Trust her and have confidence in her (Proverbs 31:11).
9. Lovingly tell your wife all the desires of your heart, practically showing your appreciation of her (Ephesians 4:29).
10. Keep yourself for your wife, devoting yourself only to her (Romans 12:10, Ephesians 5:31 and Malachi 2:15).

Chapter 9

Especially for Wives

'Wives, in the same way be submissive to your husbands so that, if any of them do not believe the word, they may be won over without words by the behaviour of their wives, when they see the purity and reverence of your lives.' (1 Peter 3:1–2)

Being a Christian is not a guarantee that your marriage will be successful. If God's principles are ignored, we are as vulnerable as the world. In this chapter I want to look at some things God says to wives.

'As the Church submits to Christ, so also wives should submit to their husbands in everything.'
(Ephesians 5:24)

Many wives say, 'I will submit to my husband in most things' or 'I will submit if I feel led to.' Neither of these statements is scriptural; many wives wish that word 'everything' were not in the Scriptures, but it is. It is there in the original Greek and in every version of the Bible I have found. The only time there is an exception is if the husband requires his wife to take part in a sinful act that specifically breaks God's law.

If a woman can honestly say, 'I submit to my husband in everything,' it is the sign of her holiness. It is not a matter of how many tracts she can give out, how many 'words of knowledge' she has received or how many meetings she attends. We read in 1 Peter 3:6 that Sarah obeyed Abraham, calling him her master.

Of course, it is possible to obey without submitting. The Bible does not say, 'Wives, obey your husbands,' it says, 'submit' to them. Submission is a condition of the heart. There is a well-known story that illustrates this difference. A father told his little child to sit. The child remained standing, so the father said again, 'Sit.' Nothing happened and angered by his child's disobedience he said, 'If you don't sit immediately, I will smack you.' As he began to walk towards his son, the boy rapidly sat down. He looked at his father and said, 'I might be sitting on the outside, but inside I am still standing up.' There was obedience, but no submission.

I believe that one of the saddest things in a marriage is for a wife to lead her husband. It dishonours God and while it might bring the wife a selfish satisfaction, it will not produce true godly harmony. God has ordained that the husband should be the head of the home. The Lord does not say that the husband is better than the wife. Personally, I would consider my wife very much better than me in many ways. But, she must fulfil her clearly defined role as the Bible has set out and I must fulfil mine; then we will have harmony. If we confuse or try to alter these roles, we will have problems. Someone has said that many wives like the plaque 'Christ is the Head of this home' because they would rather have an invisible head than a visible one! The husband is the head of the home, while Christ should be the Lord of his life.

You may argue that we are living in a different generation and that society is different. That is true, but God has not changed and He still intends the wife to submit. He created her that way. Many women look for liberty and fulfilment, but true happiness and liberty come from obeying God and the 'Makers Instructions'. Someone once said that many wives work so hard at making good husbands that they never quite manage to be good wives.

I once knew a lady in her sixties who had been married for a long time. Her husband was like a lamb and she led him everywhere. Whenever a question was addressed to her husband she answered it. I believe that is a sign of rebellion and showed what was in her heart. If you are like that, I suggest you pray that God will watch over your lips so that you do not sin with your tongue again. Of course, if your husband asks you to answer for him that is different, but be careful.

The Lord eventually got through to this lady and melted her heart. One day, at the meal table at a conference, she broke down in tears. She looked across the table at me, with tears streaming down her face. 'Don, after all these years, I can see how wrong our family has been and what mistakes I have made.' I replied, 'We are about to discover the real person God made you to be' and we did. Very quickly she became a changed woman. It is only as we come into line with God's word that we discover who we really are.

You will never discover the person God meant you to be as a wife, until you come to the place of submission. Submission does not mean that you have to be crushed or kicked around like a football. God often uses Heather to speak to me. Wives, you will often be the voice of God to your husband, but, the attitude in which you deliver the message is most important. If you try to take authority in a situation you will find yourself in trouble. For one thing, your husband will be less likely to hear what God is saying. If your spirit is right, he will listen to you. Obviously, a wife may discuss issues with her husband and should do so, but, ultimately, when it comes to making a decision he has the authority. Give him the last word. **Submission is not really tested until you disagree**. The truth is you will never discover how submissive you are until you reach that point of disagreement.

True Beauty

'Your beauty should not come from outward adornment, such as braided hair and the wearing of gold jewellery and fine clothes. Instead, it should be that of your inner self, the unfading beauty of a gentle and quiet spirit, which is of great worth in God's sight.' (1 Peter 3:3–4)

In these verses Peter talks about the appearance of a wife. Notice that Peter is not telling wives to stop using jewellery or fine clothes or presenting themselves well. I have heard people teach against using jewellery and make-up from this passage. It seems to me that the logical conclusion of that thinking is that she should not wear clothes either! No, Peter is encouraging us, 'Do not just focus on appearance; if that is all you have got, it is not enough!' A wife's attitudes are far more important than her appearance.

I believe that it is good for a wife to dress herself in ways that look good, and not to wear drab or dull clothes. It is good that she has her hair styled attractively. Heather makes sure that I like her perfume and she is not interested in wearing anything that does not appeal to me. That is one of the unselfish things a wife can do for her husband, rather than just pleasing herself. Heather will often ask me what I would like her to wear for a particular occasion. It irritates her if I say 'Wear what you like,' or 'I do not mind,' so I try to be careful to reply positively.

However, as Peter says, if the outward appearance is all that there is to a wife, there is something seriously wrong. The husband is the one who sees his wife when she wakes up dishevelled! He is not going to love her if she has nothing more to her than 'good looks'. If a husband is attracted to his wife by the holy and pure things that come out of her heart, he will not be disappointed whatever state he sees her in. The beauty of an inner godly attitude of submission will make any woman glow with the outer beauty of the glory of God.

Honesty

Peter calls a gentle and quiet spirit an incorruptible orna-
ment; yet many women I meet have an aggressive, critical
spirit. It is sad how many wives I meet openly criticise their
husbands. A husband is very blessed if he has a loyal and
faithful wife. Set your heart to be a wife that your husband
will be proud of, even if he is not a Christian. That is real
beauty.

The Amplified Bible describes the *'gentle and quiet spirit'*
as the

> *'unfading charm of a gentle and peaceful spirit which (is
> not anxious or wrought up, but) is very precious in the
> sight of God.'* (1 Peter 3:4)

Such a lady does not get anxious or ruffled when problems
come. She is in control of her emotions. Peter gives a crucial
key when he says that the holy women of old trusted in God
(1 Peter 3:5). Can you trust the Lord with your husband
and children? One of the things that I am proudest about of
Heather is that she is a woman who trusts God. During one
of our camps, when our daughter Faith was only two and a
half years old, Heather left her to play in the care of two
teenage girls. When Heather returned a few minutes later,
the girls had disappeared and a voice from above said,
'Hello, Mummy.' Faith had climbed onto the top of one of
our lorries! Calmly, Heather said, 'Faith, come down,' and
watched as she climbed down the same way that she had got
up. Trust in God has a very practical use.

A Helpmeet

The Bible says that a wife is a helpmeet for her husband.
That means that she is to support him and not hinder him.
Imagine for a moment that your husband lost his job. He
comes home and says, 'Darling, I have been made redun-
dant.' How would you respond? 'Oh dear, you can never

hold a job down?' 'Whatever will we do about the mortgage?' 'How terrible!' In times of stress, the godly response is to be a helpmeet. You can build his faith by saying, for example, 'I always knew you were worthy of a better job,' 'We will pray that you will have another one by next week,' 'I believe in you.'

A few years ago Heather and I were facing a crisis and she was the voice of God to me. She was such an encouragement. She did not express a negative word or thought but backed me all the time and was a helpmeet!

Wives should be continually responsive to their husbands, yet many fail here because they are caught up with other things. Some mothers tend to neglect their husbands because they pay so much attention to the children. I am not saying that children do not need a lot of attention; they certainly do. However, it is important to remember that your first responsibility is towards your husband. He should still have the first place in your heart. Make sure that you set aside time every day to give him your undivided attention, not just in bed.

Romance

Both husbands and wives should continue to court their partner throughout their married life. You are a special person. God made you to be romantic. If the desire for romance is missing from your life, then I believe you should go to God and ask Him to sort out your emotions. Then He can help you to become the romantic person He intends you to be. Many wives are lacking in this respect, because there was never any romance in their parent's home and they have never had a good model. However, even if you have been married for forty years and have never enjoyed romance with your partner, it does **not** mean you have missed your opportunity. God can put romance back into your marriage any time.

Be aware that the reason that many husbands look for affection from other women, is because they do not get it from their wives. I am not condoning adultery, but often it is not entirely the man's fault. Too many wives have driven their husbands into the arms of another woman because they have not given and shared the romance a husband needs. Remember, if you sit on your husband's knee, there will be no room for his secretary!

Some wives as they grow older seem to lose all interest in sex. They no longer see it as having any significance in their marriage. The result is that they leave all the initiative to their husbands. However, I am sure it is good for a marriage if the wife occasionally surprises her husband sexually.

I have met women who go around the house singing 'Hallelujah' all day and their husbands have told me that they act like an iceberg in bed! Their 'Hallelujahs' are hollow and false, masking an attitude of coldness and indifference. Charismatic prayer meetings can often be used by frustrated wives to avoid the truth; frustrated because their marriage relationship is not right. So many Christians have a pseudo-spiritual attitude that leads to staleness in their marriage relationships. God made you human, you are a sexual being. He did not make you like an angel to float around all day! God made you and gave you each other to enjoy!

To constantly use the excuse of tiredness to avoid sexual relations, is a manifestation of selfishness, which is sin. It can manifest itself in either being over-demanding or unresponsive. Are you loving your partner if you have been overworking or doing things you should not be doing and are 'too tired'? If you use sex to manipulate or bargain with your partner, that is sin too.

Food for Thought

Another way of showing love to your husband is to cook him his favourite meal. Do you know what it is? If you don't, find out and give of your best. Your husband is the greatest gift God ever gave to you, after Jesus! There is an old saying that 'a way to a man's heart is through his stomach'. I do not think that is entirely true, but it is helpful advice. In some homes, if the husband is a little late back from the office, after a long day's work, he is greeted with lack of sympathy and a cold meal. The meal has gone dry sitting in the oven, and looks less than appetizing! This is not the way to win him or keep him!

Seek to please your husband. Be the best wife possible. Have his meals ready when he gets home, if that is what he wants. It is not good to hurriedly throw a meal together just before he walks in from work; especially if the reason is that you have been out at a prayer meeting all afternoon! Your husband is more important than prayer meetings. It is your God-given ministry to care for him. Your husband and children are your number one priority. Pray with others, but do make sure your schedule reflects your priorities.

Again I would remind you that the little things count for a lot. When he arrives, meet him at the door. Be there with your arms wide open and tell him that you have missed him. Welcome him with the kind of kiss you would give him if he had been away for a month. If you pack sandwiches for his lunch, put a little love note in with them. I often find notes in my shirts when I unpack them on tour. Look after his clothes, with all the buttons on his shirts and no holes in his socks. Keep your home tidy and well presented as if the Lord Jesus himself was your guest.

Your Reverence

Finally, the wife is to reverence, honour and respect her husband. The Amplified Bible's version of Ephesians 5:33 is very interesting:

> 'Let each man of you (without exception) love his wife as [being in a sense] his very own self; and let the wife see that she respects and reverences her husband – that she notices him, regards him, honours him, prefers him,

*venerates and esteems him; and that she defers to him,
praises him, and loves and admires him exceedingly.'*

I looked at the word reverence in the original Greek. It is
only used twice in the entire Bible – once referring to God
and once to husbands. God and your husband are the only
ones who qualify to be called Reverend! To reverence
means to be 'terrified and afraid!' This is the level of
respect God expects a wife to give to her husband. It means
to have your heart in submission to him and hold him in
high esteem. Yet many wives are competing with their husbands. The hallmark of a godly, sanctified woman is that
she is in submission to her husband. Remember the chain
of authority is God, Christ, husband, wife. The way you
treat your husband is a mark of the way that you treat God.

Do you esteem your husband? Do you give him honour
and prefer him? When was the last time that you praised
him? Many Christian wives sit in the congregation looking
at their pastors or other Christian men thinking, 'I wish I
had a husband like that.' There is no man in the world like
your husband for you. God gave him to you! To disrespect
him is to show a lack of respect to God. So be careful,
because I believe there is nothing more disrespectful than to
hear a wife talking about her husband's faults to others.

Conclusion

Several years ago, a young woman heard me preach the
message of this chapter. She left the meeting very angry
and called me 'a male chauvinist pig'. Three years later I
met her at another meeting and she fell into my arms and
hugged me. She shared that she had only just got married at
the time of our first meeting. She heard me teach these
things but was convinced that her way would work. After
three years, as her marriage was falling apart and about to
collapse, she remembered my words and acted on them.
This had saved her marriage. These are the 'Maker's
Instructions'. They work, put them to the test!

As you have read this chapter, you may have recognised that something I have said is a problem in your marriage:
– Discuss it openly together.
– Make a commitment to put it right, no matter how long it takes.
– If necessary, get some help.

Chapter 10

True Liberation

'And do not be conformed to this world but be transformed by the renewing of your mind, that you may prove what is that good and acceptable and perfect will of God.'   (Romans 12:2 NKJV)

This Scripture has a special significance for us as women. It is so easy to conform to the world's standards in bringing up our children and relating to our husbands. As the world seeks to influence us, we need to turn more frequently to the 'Maker's Instructions'. We need to discover the perfect will of God for us as women.

Do you realize that a woman is not born a woman? She does not become one when she marries a man, nor when she has children or even joins the feminist rights' movement. No, a woman becomes a woman in the truest sense, when she begins to measure up to what God wants her to be. For any woman to be truly happy and fulfilled, it is necessary for her to see the plan God has for her. True happiness can only be found in Jesus Christ and in obeying His word. God made us female. but we have to learn how to become a woman.

Many women look for liberty and fulfilment, but as someone has rightly stated: 'Just as a room is not a room

without walls, so liberty is not liberty without boundaries.'
Our boundary is the Word of God. Some women feel that if
they accept the Bible's teaching for wives, they will forfeit
their own personality or standing. That is a lie! True happiness means discovering and fulfilling God's plan for us.
Every woman is wonderfully made and designed by God to
give pleasure. I believe that this is the fundamental principle
of femininity. Woman was made to complement man (in
the words of the Amplified Bible). Usually when we think
about the word 'complement' we mean something that
enhances the object it is placed with. We were made to
complete man. Part of this completing is to bring pleasure,
for example in companionship and friendship. For those
of us who are married it will be first to our husband and
then to others including our children. So often women are
only regarded as present to reproduce and as an object to
satisfy sexual desire, but I believe that God intended more
for us as women. We can be freed from the bondages that
are placed on us in this way and then be at liberty to give
our husbands all that God intended so that we do truly
complete them.

We are liberated when we break free from competitiveness and jealousy. Those who advocate 'the women's movement' and 'equal rights for women' have stirred up an
unhealthy competitive spirit between men and women. The
assumption that men automatically put women down, and
women have to struggle free from men's dominance has
now become the 'normal' way to live, even in the Church.
God never intended that there should be competitiveness
between any human beings.

If we go back to the account of creation, we see that God

> *'created man in His **own** image, in the image of God He
> created him; male and female He created them.'*
> (Genesis 1:27 NKJV)

It is as though God cut Himself in two, putting part of
Himself in man and part in women. Into the male He put

certain characteristics, such as strength, protectiveness, and leadership. Into the female He put tenderness, sensitivity and an ability to express creativity in a way men can not, among other things. Together, a husband and wife team can really complement each other and are better equipped to show forth the image of God.

Not Inferior

God made Adam first and then He made Eve. Because she came second that does not mean that she was inferior. Remember that Christ is called *'the last Adam'* and the *'second man'* (1 Corinthians 15:45 and 47). Adam came first and Christ second, but there is no question that the second Adam was greater than the first. So the woman is not inferior because she was made after man. But she is different; the woman was made to complement the man and complete the partnership. The Bible tells us that *'woman is the glory of man'* (1 Corinthians 11:7). If we can really see this and accept it, it will change our attitude to being a woman. This is especially true as we seek to fulfil our roles of wife and mother.

Time to Adapt

'The head of every man is Christ, the head of woman, is man, and the head of Christ is God.'

In 1 Corinthians 11:3 we are given God's order for mankind. In the world this order has been rejected and the wrong attitude has spilled into the church. There are so many Christian women, especially single young ladies, who get uptight about the subject of submission and obedience.

Many women who get married say, 'I am going to be myself. I have always been like this; this is the way I intend to carry on.' The Amplified Bible says in Ephesians 5:22,

> *'Wives ... adapt yourselves – to your own husbands as [a service] to the Lord.'*

To produce harmony in your marriage, it is important that you adapt yourself to your husband. As wives we must be prepared to adjust. This does not mean that our husbands are totally right or that they do not have to change. However, it is our responsibility to make sure that our part of the marriage relationship is working right. We need to look for areas in our lives where we can change and adapt. Do not point the finger and say, 'If he changes, so will I.' To be truly one with our partner, we must adapt to our partner's likes and dislikes.

Too many women marry with the idea that they are going to change their partner because they do not like this or that about him. If you got married with that attitude, look at yourself and remember the words of Jesus

> *'first take the plank out of your own eye, and then you will see clearly to remove the speck from your brother's eye.'* (Matthew 7:5)

Recognise that there are things about you that your partner may dislike and resolve to change them. If we can see that we are complementing our husbands, we will add to him and not take away. The result will be that we will bring out in him things that other people have not seen; we shall add to the richness of his manhood and at the same time begin to fulfil our womanhood.

Are you married to a minister or church leader? If you are, have you been called to this work yourself? The point of this question relates to submission. If you are forced to be involved in your husband's ministry but feel no calling yourself to it, you will have problems in submission. I challenge you to seek the Lord so that you know with certainty that you know His calling; you should be in the ministry together. I do not believe that the Lord would call a wife to a separate ministry, because God has made you one, and you should minister as one.

Don and I, kneeling at the communion rail in a small church, dedicated ourselves to serve the Lord together; it was a very precious moment in our relationship. We settled it there, the Lord and His call on our lives would come first in our relationship. We committed ourselves, whether together or apart, to doing the will of God. That included the times when Don was ministering on the other side of the world and I was at home with the family. Thirty years later, we look back on that day as the point that brought stability into our relationship. We never allow our overwhelming love for each other to interfere with the top priority, which is the call and gifting of God. Occasionally I have had to be very firm with Don when he's been reluctant to go on a ministry trip without me. We are both totally committed to the will and call of God on our lives.

True Submission

From the day we were married I have always wanted to be in submission to Don. I am not a 'yes' person and I do voice my opinions. If I feel that he is making a wrong decision or taking a wrong course of action I will tell him so. However, my submission means that having talked it through, I will gladly do what he decides. I do not oppose him. In my dictionary, the word 'submit' is defined as 'to arrange your life under another's.' As wives we have to arrange our lives under those of our husbands.

If a woman submits in love to her husband, it will release his love towards you. He will also begin to exercise his God-given authority and protective instincts. A once harsh husband can become strong and loving, because he no longer needs to be on the defensive to prove himself. Get right behind your husband and seek to make him a successful leader in every respect.

Some women say 'What do I lose if I do not obey?' The first thing that goes is protection. If we are obedient to authority, that will bring protection from pressure. God has ordained that we as women should have this protection, not only for own sakes, but also for the testimony of Jesus Christ. We should desire to reflect the beauty of submission in our lives.

No matter how long we have been married or who our husbands are, we are to submit to them. Note that we are to be in submission to our husbands. There are many other figures of authority in our lives – church leaders, parents, work bosses, but our husband is the one we are to submit to. If there is a 'clash' our husband's will must take priority.

As to the Lord

The Bible does not say submit to your husband only if he is right. When we submit to our husband, we are not just submitting to a man; first we are submitting to God. The Bible tells us to submit *'as to the Lord'* (Ephesians 5:22 KJV).

Submission is not gritting your teeth and saying, 'I must submit because God says so.' True submission must become such an attitude in your heart that often you do not realize that it is what you are doing. There is only one occasion when we are not to obey our husbands, and that is if they ask us to do something that violates God's Word. This is the only exception. Every other time, God requires us to submit. There have been times when Don has asked me to do something and I have disagreed but have then obeyed. Even when we submit feeling that the decision is wrong, God is always going to vindicate His Word and work the situation out for our own good. Our submission is to the Lord, who rules, and because He rules, He can overrule in His own unique way if a husband should be wrong. With that kind of faith, we have confidence in our submission.

I once heard someone comment that the Bible teaches that the woman is an underdog or a slave. How can that possibly be? A woman can never be in such an inferior role when she is in the place that God wants her to be. Behind every successful marriage is a woman, upholding and backing her man. The Lord can use the most ill-equipped husband to guide a submissive wife, simply because she supports his delegated authority. When a woman is secure under her husband's authority, she may be more adventurous than her sister who imagines herself to be without restraint.

A major key to getting submission right is trust. If you know that your husband loves you, you can freely submit, knowing that he has your interests at heart.

I believe that we should be united on every point. That means sharing with one another; share your thoughts and the way you feel about an issue. At home, when I cannot reach Don and have to make a decision, I say to myself, 'Well, what would Don do?' If I am unsure, I will contact one of our elders from the church and ask for their covering for the decisions I make. It is essential that you teach your family that your husband is the head of the home. If your children come and ask you something that is a decision your husband should make, send them to him.

There are times too, when you should tell your children that you need to be alone with your husband. On no account should your children be allowed to come between you and your husband. This however, needs to be done sensitively, so that you do not produce a feeling of being unwanted. We need to take time to teach them how to be sensitive to other people's needs. A typical example is the period after their father comes home from work after a tiring day and needs time to relax and unwind.

Home Truths

The husband is the head of the home, but you are the one who has to create the atmosphere in the home. It is up to you to create a good environment for your family. Send your children to school with a happy image of Mum. Wives, send your husbands to work with a happy image of you, so that they will have someone they want to come home to.

113

> *'Admonish the young women to love their husbands, to love their children, to be discreet, chaste, homemakers, good, obedient to their own husbands, that the word of God may not be blasphemed.'*   (Titus 2:4–5 NKJV)

So often the world can point a finger at the Church because of what it sees in Christians' lives. We often bring dishonour and discredit on the Gospel because of the way we live. Paul told Titus to teach women to be *'discreet, chaste, homemakers.'* I was brought up very strictly. Our family attended church meetings three times on a Sunday and most nights of the week. Yet my mother kept the home clean and tidy, meals were always properly served and my father was always adequately cared for.

At 17, the Lord called me to serve Him, and I began travelling the country. When I started staying in other Christian homes, I was shocked with what I saw. I met some women who got up in the morning, and without making the beds and washing the dishes, went out all day to prayer meetings or visiting friends. When their husbands came home, nothing had been done in the house. That, in my view, dishonoured the Gospel.

If I am ever at home and feel the Lord wants me to deal with a situation in the church or team, my priority is still my home. I will give the issue to the Lord until I have finished the work I have to do. I do not accept the idea that God will tell me to leave the washing up and visit Mrs X (unless there is a real emergency); God is big enough to keep the situation until I have fulfilled the duties in my home first.

See Jesus in your husband and family. After all, if your husband is saved, Jesus lives in him. What would you do with your home if Jesus was going to live there? He is there anyway, whether you consciously realize it or not.

> *'Whatever you do – no matter what it is – in word or deed, do everything in the name of the Lord Jesus **and** in*

[dependence upon] His Person, giving praise to God the Father through Him.'
(Colossians 3:17 The Amplified Bible)

We should cook meals, wash clothes, clean and tidy for our husbands, as if we were doing it for Jesus. It makes a real difference if you see the so called 'mundane' tasks, as done for the Lord. Jesus said

'I tell you the truth, whatever you did for one of the least of these brothers of mine, you did for me.'
(Matthew 25:40)

Suppose Jesus was coming to live with you. Are there things in your home you would want to change? Then change them, because He is living with you, all the time, in your husband, in your family, and in yourself.

Here are some practical applications we can make:

Prepare a daily rota, jobs to be done by certain times. Modern psychologists have found that the most successful business people often use lists to guide their work. It works as successfully in the home as in the business world. Plan both weekly and monthly job lists, and do things in an organised way.

There is a saying, 'Cleanliness is next to godliness.' There is no need for a Christian home ever to be dirty. Have the children looking clean and tidy when your husband comes home, so that he can be proud of them.

Being a mother and wife is a life of servanthood, but not slavery. Take some time now to consider what I have said in this chapter and allow the Lord to put His finger on the areas where change is needed.

Chapter 11

Redeemed from the Curse

As women, we often find ourselves living in victory three weeks of every month. In the fourth week down we go – out for the count, defeated, depressed and dejected. It takes some women a whole week to regain the victory, get free from condemnation and start 'living' again. God never intended us to be like this.

> 'To the woman He said: "I will greatly multiply your sorrow and your conception; In pain you shall bring forth children; Your desire shall be for your husband, And he shall rule over you."'   (Genesis 3:16 NKJV)

Here is the beginning of all this suffering. Because of Adam and Eve's sin, God put a curse on Eve that every woman has had to suffer since then. You may see this clearly, but simply understanding does not remove the problems we have to face each month. Since *'Christ has redeemed us from the curse of the law'* (Galatians 3:13), is it necessary to live in the shadow of another person's sin? A study of Romans, chapters 4, 5 and 6 give us a clearer picture of our redemption from the curse and the law. Adam sinned and we all fell! Jesus died that we may **all** live in victory over the results of Adam's sin.

Let's look at Genesis 3:16 in more detail. God said he would multiply your sorrow and your conception. To multiply you need a basis to start from, i.e. $2 \times 2 = 4$. There is a basis for our discomfort; of necessity, there is the sensation of our seed producing itself and starting its course. It is this sensation that has been greatly multiplied. Why? Simply, because of the effects of sin. This is the reason for all the symptoms that so many of us experience: depression, abnormal pain, water retention, an imbalance of hormones, etc. The good news is that we can be free from all these. We don't need healing, we need to be set free from the effects of sin. As we recognize what Jesus purchased for us on the cross we can be released. Most of us have experienced the benefits of this in part. For example we know freedom from the power of sin, guilt, and condemnation. Yet we still stay bound by Satan in this area, believing we have to suffer, and our families along with us.

The same principle applies to the next part of Genesis 3:16, *'In pain you shall bring forth children.'* Again, there is a basic pain a woman will experience in giving birth to a child; this pain has been multiplied by the effect of sin that entered the world when Adam and Eve rebelled. The contractions necessary to bring a child to birth are painful. However, the intense pain and the complications that so many people teach us to expect, are not what God planned when He made us.

The Bible tells us that we shall be saved in childbirth if we *'continue in faith, love, and holiness, with self control'* (1 Timothy 2:15 NKJV). Notice this freedom is conditional upon us continuing in faith, love, holiness and self control. In other words, it is all tied up to our relationship with God. We do not annul God's Word by our experience, but we should seek to make God's Word our present experience. God has made provision for us to live in victory in all parts of our life. He did this through the cross of Jesus Christ. It is here we must look for victory and deliverance from the curse.

My mother nearly lost her life when both my brother and I were born. Each labour lasted for two days. The doctor told me that this would happen to me. Don and I got before the Lord and claimed God's promises in the Bible and I experienced complete freedom. In fact, the healthiest times of my life have been when expecting and bearing children.

[A fuller consideration of the effects of the Curse on women can be found in Heather's book *Twentieth Century Eve*, Nova 1990.]

Darling, I Love You

Let's think a little about the subject of loving our husbands. So many wives wonder why they are sexually frustrated and I believe the answer lies at this point. God designed us so that we need the release of a good marital relationship. Because the clock strikes 'bedtime', it does not mean now is the time to start showing love to your husband. You should have been loving him all day long. Love his good points and his bad points, his thoughts and his frustrations, listen to his plans and ideas. Compliment him, physically touch him and in different ways show your feelings for him. Then your relationship at night will be fulfilling and not just a 'duty'.

Experiment with different ways of expressing your love to him. Do you remember the little ways you used to attract him when you were courting? Do things that say 'Darling, I love you.' As the years go by, romance is something that so often fades in marriages. This should not be so, it should grow, mature and become more precious. If the little things that used to be so special have gone from your experience, try to recover them.

Problems sometimes arise from partners wanting to make love at different times of the day. For example, one partner may prefer love-making at night, while the other favours the morning when feeling refreshed from a good night's sleep. These things present an opportunity for showing consideration and unselfish love.

> *'The wife does not have authority over her own body, but the husband does. And likewise the husband does not have authority over his own body, but the wife does. Do not deprive one another except with consent for a time, that you may give yourselves to fasting and prayer; and come together again so that Satan does not tempt you because of your lack of self-control.'*
>
> (1 Corinthians 7:4-5 NKJV)

A legalistic response to this verse, that of having intercourse out of a sense of duty, is not enough. There needs to be a loving response from the heart, which God can give you. If you deprive your husband in the realm of your sexual relationship, you may cause him to be tempted. When a husband has extra-marital relationships, it is often as much the wife's fault as his. You have a responsibility before God for your husband to see that he is sexually fulfilled.

Always find time to listen to your husband and to hear his plans and ideas about his job. It is your responsibility to compliment him. You should be the first one, next to God, that your husband turns to. Some men look outside their marriage because their wives will not listen to them.

Keep Your Husband

How does your home compare to his office? That may sound an odd question because they are two very different places, but think about it. Many offices are very organised, with efficient secretaries who dress smartly, and work hard at creating the right impression. What is your home like? It doesn't matter if you go out to work as well, or don't work because you have children to care for – the same questions apply and need answering. Does your home look uncared for and untidy? When your husband comes home from work what does he expect to find? Obviously mothers with small children have a full-time job caring for them, but it does not mean that everything else must be neglected. Your appearance, your children's appearance, and what the house looks like must be welcoming and communicate 'we are glad you're home.' While there is no excuse for a man who breaks the commitment he made when he got married, a wife does have a great influence on the chances of him having an affair. By making an effort, you can hold his attention and his eyes won't wander!

Dressed for the Occasion

> *'Also [I desire] that the woman should adorn themselves modestly **and** appropriately and sensibly in seemly apparel, not with [elaborate] hair arrangement or gold or pearls or expensive clothing.'*
>
> (1 Timothy 2:9 The Amplified Bible)

In this Scripture we read of a woman's outward appearance, how God wants us to look. We should dress:

Modestly – The Oxford English Dictionary defines this as 'being inconspicuous'. I believe this can mean not being flamboyant or loud but dressing modestly in a way that glorifies God.

Appropriately – For example, if you were going for a country walk on a farm, it would be inappropriate to wear an evening blouse, full-length dress and lots of jewellery. If you were to be presented to the Queen at Buckingham Palace, it would not be appropriate for you to wear a pair of dirty, torn jeans. To dress appropriately means to wear clothes that suit the occasion.

Sensibly in seemly apparel – For me, this includes not wearing extremely short skirts and low-cut dresses.

I believe that the God whom I represent is worthy of my best. My husband and family, whom I love are also worthy of my best. No husband, parent, or child wishes to be associated with a woman who is habitually unkempt or careless in appearance.

Young women need to be taught to be real ladies. Femininity is one attribute of a Christian woman that has generally been lost in our society. In Deuteronomy 22:5 we read,

> '*A woman shall not wear anything that pertains to a man, nor shall a man put on a woman's garment, for all who do so are an abomination to the* LORD *your God.*'
>
> (NKJV)

I remember as a teenager seeing a woman I knew quite well, who dressed as a man. She wore a man's suit, socks and shoes. Everything about her was manly. Her whole attitude was that of a man and this is what God is dealing with in this verse. I believe we should be able to tell at a glance the gender of a person. We must teach young women to dress and present themselves in a way that enhances their femininity.

I do not think we can tell our young people that they should not follow the fashions of today. Providing the latest 'in' craze is not an immodest one, they can use the current fashions and still be godly men and women. How we dress expresses the attitude of our heart, therefore if our heart is truly righteous towards God, it will be expressed in the way we dress.

As a wife, can you see areas of weakness in your life in what I have said? I would challenge you to deal with those weaknesses. The result will be happiness greater than you ever thought possible and the blessing of God on your home.

Ten Commandments for Wives

1. Love the Lord your God with all your heart, mind, soul and strength and your husband only a little less than you love God (Deuteronomy 6:5).
2. Gladly submit to your husband, as to the Lord (Ephesians 5:22).
3. Be diligent to keep your tongue controlled. Be careful to bless and encourage your husband verbally at least

once a day and never discuss with others intimate details about your love relationships (Proverbs 31:26, 11:16).

4. Keep a joyful heart in all that your daily schedule calls you to do (Colossians 3:17).
5. Don't allow jealousy or selfishness be a part of your nature (Proverbs 6:34).
6. Be diligent to keep yourself and your home, attractive. Remember that you must not only win your husband's love but keep it (Proverbs 31:27 & 28).
7. Prefer your husband; never compare him unfavourably with other men. Sincerely admire and honour him (Ephesians 5:33).
8. Prize your womanly virtues and value them more than life itself (Proverbs 12:4).
9. Instil in your children love, respect and devotion for their father (Proverbs 22:6).
10. Do not nag (Proverbs 24:24, 27:15).

PART THREE

Making a Family

Chapter 12

Fatherhood

'The righteous man leads a blameless life; blessed are his children after him.' (Proverbs 20:7)

The God-given role of 'parent' is one of the highest callings in the Kingdom of God. Bringing up children can be the most enjoyable, fulfilling and rewarding of experiences. In the chapters that follow, we are going to look at the relationship God wants parents to have with their children. We trust that you will be challenged and encouraged to go for the best.

In Proverbs 20:7, it is important to note that your lifestyle will have a direct result on the development of your children. God makes a specific promise to the man (and that includes both male and female) who lives with integrity. God will bless the children of such a man. The best thing we can do for our children is to become totally sold out to God. As we seek to serve Him and to fulfil His will, plan and purpose in our lives our children will get the benefits. Sadly, I meet many people who compromise on God's words and plans; the result is that not only do they lose out, but their family does as well.

Our Heavenly Father is the perfect model of fatherhood. If you want to see what a good father is like, just look at your Father in heaven. It is true that how we were humanly fathered will often affect the relationship we have with

Father God. Bad memories and reactions to our natural fathers need dealing with; it may be necessary to seek prayer and counsel to get free from those past hurts.

A Good Image

I regularly meet people who think of God as someone 'hiding around the next corner with a big stick' waiting to catch them out. This produces a horribly distorted fear of God, and it can usually be traced back to an experience from childhood. Your Heavenly Father wants to set you free from wrong fears of Him so that you can know Him as 'Dad'. It is important that you get this sorted out, because how you were fathered will affect how you father your own children.

I stay in many people's homes as I travel. One thing I have noticed is that there are men called 'Father' who never do the things a father should do. Just because you have the title doesn't make you a father, because true fathering is all about a relationship. What comes out of that relationship is the fruit of what we put into it.

When my eldest son, Nigel, became a father for the first time, he did something that impressed me. His son Matthew was born in the early hours of the morning so Nigel had been up for most of the night at the hospital. Early in the morning he came back to stay with us while his wife and baby were still in the hospital. At 8.00 am I found him studying his Bible; I thought he was going to bed to catch up on the sleepless night. He explained that he was doing a Bible study on being a father. He said, 'I've never been one before, and I want to find out what the Bible has to say about it.'

Nigel is a good father because he took the trouble to find out what the Bible has to say and then applied it. I would like to recommend to every father reading this book, do a study on what the Word of God says about fathering. It will change you and your family will get blessed.

I have said that we need to look to God as our model of

the Perfect Father. How do you do that? Jesus was asked the same question:

> '"I am the way and the truth and the life. No one comes to the Father except through me. If you really knew me, you would know my Father as well. From now on, you do know him and have seen him." Philip said, "Lord, show us the Father and that will be enough for us." Jesus answered: "Don't you know me, Philip, even after I have been among you such a long time? Anyone who has seen me has seen the Father. How can you say, 'Show us the Father'? Don't you believe that I am in the Father, and that the Father is in me? The words I say to you are not just my own. Rather, it is the Father, living in me, who is doing his work. Believe me when I say that I am in the Father and the Father is in me; or at least believe on the evidence of the miracles themselves."'*   (John 14:6–11)

When we look at Jesus, we discover what the Father is like. Jesus came to show us the Father. He was made in the likeness of man, like you and me, so that He could reveal to us what the Father is like. It is true, the more I get to know Jesus, the more I know the Father.

Fathering is not a hobby, it's one of the most important callings that a man can choose. It is a choice in the sense that we all choose to have children and to become fathers. It is a very important decision to make; if other commitments take our time and energy we need to be careful. If they stop us fulfilling our calling as fathers then our priorities must change.

Children are God's special gift to us. Do you thank God for them? Our attitudes are expressed in our actions and priorities. Take a good look at them, it will tell you what you think of the gift God has given you.

> 'Sons are a heritage from the LORD, children a reward from him.'   (Psalm 127:3)

Even at three in the morning, when they have been sick, or are teething, or have wet the bed, children are a reward! All of us go through the night time experiences so look at them as opportunities for God to shape your character.

Authority and Order

'For the husband is the head of the wife as Christ is the head of the church, his body, of which he is the Saviour.'
(Ephesians 5:23)

God has invested the authority of the home in the father and we must accept that responsibility. Don't try to pass the buck onto your wife. God has not invested the authority in the mother because He has put some very different gifts into the woman. They are wonderful gifts that we should all respect and recognise as such. However, authority is given to fathers and you need to be clear on how that works because it will be challenged. Your children will try to divide you and your wife. Let me give you an example:

'Dad, can I borrow the car?'

'No, not today.'

Five minutes later you hear 'Mum, can I borrow the car?' Without knowing you said no, she says 'Yes.'

If you have older teenagers, does that sound familiar? Your authority will be challenged so it is important that you respond quickly. It may not be using the car, but buying sweets, or bed time extensions or going out to play. Be aware that your children need to know that you and your wife are one; if they try to divide you, make it clear that you won't allow it.

You are responsible for discipling your family, not the church. If church is working well, that is biblically, it should be discipling the fathers in it. Every father is then responsible for the spiritual growth of their family. I can always tell how good a father is by having a good look at his children. Dads, if you want to know how well you are doing, take a good look at your children. It may be a painful thing to do, but if the pain turns into a heart change that affects the way we exercise our responsibility, it will be worthwhile.

Sunday School, Junior Church and young peoples' groups have a role to play in the development of your child. However, it is **not** their job to care for your child's spiritual growth. It is your responsibility as parents, and primarily the father's. Are you teaching your children the Word of God? Fathers, we have a responsibility to sow the Word of God into our children and one day God will call us to account for what we do. Don't say, 'It is too late, they're teenagers.' It is never too late; you can adjust and change but you've got to believe it is worthwhile.

In our home we have tried to read the Bible and pray with the children regularly. I have preached the gospel to my children and to my grandchildren from the day they were born. It is possible, I believe, to sow the seed of God's Word into a child's spirit from the day they are born. Even as they have laid in their cots I have told them, 'Jesus died on the cross for you. You're going to have your sins forgiven, and be converted at an early age.' It works; every one of them was saved while still young. What you sow is what you reap, and if you don't sow good seed you won't reap good fruit.

Judson Cornwall once said,

'It is easy to leave the character development of our children to God, to the Church or to chance, but God gives that responsibility to parents.'

Parents, we must teach moral values to our children. Many people in this generation are lawless by nature because as children they were not taught things like submission to authority and righteous relationships with others. As the life of Samson proves, no amount of divine anointing can replace moral values and true inner character.

You may think that it is easier to say, than do. How do you put it into practice? One important way is for a father to become a friend to his children. My children are my friends. I value friendship very highly and make it a priority to build those relationships. Friendships with your children cost, they are time consuming, take effort and sacrifice, but are 'worth the world'. If you have got children that are proving difficult, give them your friendship and don't look for anything back. If you look for a two-way friendship immediately, you will be disappointed. Learn to reach out to them and in the end you'll reap a reward.

Passing On Truth

It's important that we express our own convictions, especially about what we believe and what the Bible says. Take time to explain to your children what you believe, never assume they will understand if you don't tell them. As they grow up and have to make decisions for themselves, if you have shown them how you have developed your beliefs, they will come and discuss things with you. Be honest with them and they will be honest with you. It is an exciting day when a child says 'Dad, I believe this now, what do you think?' I don't want my children to be clones of Don Double; I want them to have backbone and strength of character so they can make decisions on their own. God is a God who created variety and it is a privilege to teach your children to appreciate different tastes.

If you have strong convictions, teach them to your children, because if you don't teach them television will. I don't expect television to shape the lives of my children. Sometimes I have found they have been watching programmes I don't like, and so I try to make it clear to them why I disapprove. It isn't a question of shouting 'turn it off, now!' You need to discuss the issue with them; show them that you have a reason for your conviction.

Our beliefs shape our thinking and attitudes; it is important therefore, that as we help our children form their beliefs we also pay attention to their attitudes. Their motivations are perhaps more important than their actions. For too long we have concentrated on what people do, which ultimately leads to legalism, instead of finding out why they do it. As one commentator said 'our children may have the right answers but the wrong attitudes.' We need to be careful to pay attention to the attitudes we teach our children and our example is of course Jesus:

> *'Your attitude should be the same as that of Christ Jesus.'*   (Philippians 2:5)

I believe we should nurture those internal motivations that will make our children honour Jesus Christ, live responsibly, productively and be concerned for others. That obviously flows from a relationship with the Lord Jesus Christ. In the end, that is what will produce good husbands, wives, fathers and mothers.

Chapter 13

Happy Fathers – Happy Families

When each of us is born again, our relationship with God changes. **He** does not change, but begins a father–child relationship with each of us; this is something all of us need, but we don't experience it until we become followers of Jesus.

> 'Because you are sons, God sent the Spirit of his Son into our hearts, the Spirit who calls out, "Abba, Father."'
>
> (Galatians 4:6)

Many people struggle to relate to God as Father because they have never known what a real father is like. As one person put it, 'Talking to me about a father is like speaking to me in a foreign language.' It is hardly surprising that some people feel like this, when you look at the divorce statistics and the general breakdown of family life. Many of today's young people have never known a true father–child relationship; the word 'father' only stirs memories of pain and hurt, instead of the feelings of comfort and assurance that it should bring.

Our understanding of fatherhood must come from God, not from the world. The media in particular, often presents a false picture of 'father' figures, which can adversely affect family life. For instance, next time you see a TV programme, especially a sit-com, with a 'father' in the cast, notice carefully how he is portrayed. You will probably find the image presented is at variance with the teaching in God's Word.

God's Word is the only source of reliable information we have on what a father should be and do. Our supreme example is God himself, 'the Father of us all'. The best way for a child to learn about fatherhood is from a father who models himself upon the character of God.

Everyone needs a father figure in their lives, not just children. I am convinced that there is a desperate lack of 'fathers in God' today. Many people can echo the words of Philip, *'Lord, show us the Father'* (John 14:8). As I said in the previous chapter I believe that fatherhood on earth is important to help people understand and relate to God as their Father. Paul said both to individuals and whole churches that they were to take him as a 'model'. He also told the Christians at Corinth,

> *'Even though you have ten thousand guardians in Christ, you do not have many fathers, for in Christ Jesus I became your father through the gospel.'*
>
> (1 Corinthians 4:15)

To be a father means to provide love, security, leadership, affection, acceptance and comfort for your children. In this chapter we will look at some aspects of fathering and how they affect family life. Everyone needs to experience the love of a human father. People of all ages, children and adults, often come up to me and say, 'Mr Double, will you give me a "father hug"? I have never had one before.' I trust that as you read this chapter you will get a good look of God's design for fathers.

Fatherly Love

Being a father is far more than a title that is given to one member of a family. Relationship is at the core. To be a father is to be more than just a 'guardian'. God wants to

> *'turn the hearts of the fathers to their children, and the hearts of the children to their fathers.'* (Malachi 4:6)

> *'There is no fear in love. But perfect love drives out fear, because fear has to do with punishment. The one who fears is not made perfect in love.'* (1 John 4:18)

The Psalmist described God's love as *'better than life'* (Psalm 63:3). Trust and love are two qualities that go hand in hand. As you understand that someone loves you, then you can begin to build bridges of trust. There should be no fear in a father–child relationship. Every child needs to know that they can come and talk anything through with their father without being afraid.

As one commentator has said, 'your children need to know you love them and that is spelt T-I-M-E.' Children need to know that dad's ear is always available, that he will listen and justly consider what they say, even if he might say 'no' to a request. Many fathers are austere, hard, religious, or just too busy to sit and listen. Consequently many young people get into a mess because they were not able to talk through issues with their parents. Give yourself to your children so they know they have someone who belongs to them.

Fatherly Security

Many years ago I heard a song in which were these words:

> 'He loves you when you're right,
>   and He loves you when you're wrong.'

That is God's attitude to us in a nutshell; it is also how we should be with each other. I will love my children whatever I discover about them. My love for them is never on the line! As I find a person has failed or sinned deeply, somehow I feel that they need my love more.

Every child needs to know that there is a place in the

family that belongs to them. A place that is their size, has their name on it, a place which nobody else can take away. With my own father, however much trouble I got in, he was always there. I thank God for that. I have never had a problem relating to God as Father, because of my father's example.

Fatherly Discipline

Discipline is vital, but it must come out of love, or it will not produce its goal – maturity. Loving discipline should be aimed at deepening your relationship. It seems that every time I disciplined my children, our relationship and their love for me grew. More than one of my extended family came to me and said, 'If I need discipline, please give it to me.' (They were all in their late teens and twenties.) Some of them grew up without regular, loving discipline and they realised that there was something lacking in their lives. Godly discipline, grounded in love, will produce security in your children. We will take a fuller look at discipline in family life in a later chapter.

Fatherly Leadership

Then Jesus came to them and said,

> *'All authority in heaven and on earth has been given to me.'* (Matthew 28:18)

As we have already considered, the Lord has delegated His authority to the husband to be the head and leader of the home. A father who does not make use of this authority will be weak and ineffective.

While I was away from home, my children related to Heather for everything, but, the moment I walked through the door Heather deferred to my authority. She would tell the children 'Dad is home now, go to him.' A father who leads, will be a father who is respected by his children.

138

Fatherly Fun

I believe that God wants us to have fun and relax and laugh together. Many Christian homes I visit are too 'super spiritual' and intense for that to happen. Psalm 2 says

> *'The One enthroned in heaven laughs.'*   (Psalm 2:4)

While you may argue about the meaning of the context of that scripture, I believe that it reveals a side of God's character few of us think about. God has a sense of humour and He put it into man when He created us. The ability to smile and laugh and enjoy good company are all things we need to develop in our families. There is a well-known statement, 'The family that prays together stays together.' It is equally true to say that 'The family that **plays** together, stays together.' Times of fun are important.

In the story of the Prodigal son (Luke 15), the father celebrated the return of his younger son with a party. Our children need the opportunity to celebrate from time to time. As a family we often have a party, just for the sake of it; you don't need to wait until it is someone's birthday! Too many Christians think that God is a big man in the sky with a stick, with a stern frown on His face and no sense of fun. Fathers, we have to change this wrong idea and one way we can help is by partying. I am looking forward to the wedding reception that is promised in Revelation 19. I doubt that it will a sombre affair, I am convinced that it will be an incredible celebration, filled with enjoyment and delight. Get hold of some of that now and enjoy your family.

As a family we developed this idea into our 'Family Nights'. Each month we set aside one evening, which was just for us. It was an undisturbed evening (which often meant not answering the telephone), when everyone in the family made a contribution to the evening. Someone was allowed to choose their favourite thing to eat, another would choose an activity or game, and so on. The children looked forward to these times because they were fun and they had Mum and Dad's undivided attention.

Fun is an important key to growing a healthy family; yet so many parents are too 'super-spiritual', or afraid of losing respect if they 'let their hair down'. The truth is that instead of losing respect you will gain it. I remember one incident very vividly: we were reading from Proverbs during our family devotions and sharing what the Lord had said to us from the passage. Faith, who was ten at the time, quoted the verse,

> *'A wise son brings joy to his father, but a foolish son grief to his mother.'* (Proverbs 10:1)

I asked her how this verse applied to her and how she could 'make her father glad.' I expected her to answer 'by being wise and not foolish' but she said, 'to play with him and tickle his feet,' which she promptly did!

For us, 'Family Nights' have changed and developed as the children have got older, but they have been an important part of our life together. Whatever we chose to do or eat, it was a good opportunity to teach sharing and *'preferring one another'*; everyone learnt to get fully involved, even if it was not their 'thing'. Your financial circumstances may make you feel you can't do a special meal, or go out to do something together, but, there is one thing we have all got – **time**. None of us have more or less than anyone else. How we use it is our choice. Give some to your family and you will discover some rich rewards.

Family holidays have always been a very precious time for us. Because of who I am, we have tried to go somewhere where we are unknown, although that hasn't always worked! Family holidays are times for me to give myself 100% to the family. I count it a great privilege as a father to be able to serve the rest of the family when we are on holiday; especially to give my wife a break from the routine chores.

I also seek to take each of my children out on their own

from time to time. Family activities are very important, but each child also needs time with their father for themselves.

Fatherly Provision

The Bible tells us that our heavenly Father knows the things we need, so we do not have to worry about them. He promises that as we seek first His Kingdom and righteousness, all sorts of things will be given to us (Matthew 6:32–33).

> *'If you, then, though you are evil, know how to give good gifts to your children, how much more will your Father in heaven give good gifts to those who ask him!'*
>
> (Matthew 7:11)

I would get the top brick off the chimney for any of my children if they needed it! If I, being 'evil', would do that, just think of our heavenly Father's goodness;

> *'He who did not spare his own Son, but gave him up for us all how will he not also, along with him, graciously give us all things?'*   (Romans 8:32)

So many people have the idea that God is stingy. God radically changed this thinking in me one day as I was driving down the M1. I was enjoying the Lord by myself, when He spoke to me, in a fatherly way. He said, 'Don, why won't you let me love you the way I want to?' I thought I did, so I said so. He quickly replied, 'I want to love you far more than that. You haven't really begun yet.' Then God said to me 'I have given you a nice car to drive; yet, when people talk to you about it, you try to justify it.' I had to confess that was true. When people asked me why I owned an expensive car, I would say I needed a comfortable, reliable car. My reason was I drive long distances and then preach, and so don't want to be tired when I get there. God said to me, 'Why don't you just say, "My Father loves me"?' As I thought about it, it released something in me,

141

and I pray that you come to the same place too. Our Father loves us, passionately, and wants to bless us, abundantly.

Look again at the Father's response when his wayward son returned,

> *'So he got up and went to his father. But while he was still a long way off, his father saw him and was filled with compassion for him; he ran to his son, threw his arms around him and kissed him … But the father said to his servants, "Quick! Bring the best robe and put it on him. Put a ring on his finger and sandals on his feet. Bring the fattened calf and kill it. Let's have a feast and celebrate. For this son of mine was dead and is alive again; he was lost and is found." So they began to celebrate.'* (Luke 15:20, 22–24)

I think that we could describe that as extravagant love. The best robe, a fattened calf, servants running about to fulfil their master's orders; the Father wanted a great celebration for his son's return. When was the last time you gave your children a party, a proper 'knees-up'? Please don't wait until they are 'the returned prodigal' before you do it. One thing I have learnt with my own children is that I will never lose my children by giving them a party, often the reverse. Blessing my children is a joy; accept that your Heavenly Father wants to bless you and your family in greater measure.

If a child lives with criticism – He learns to condemn.
If a child lives with hostility – He learns to fight.
If a child lives with ridicule – He learns to be shy.
If a child lives with shame – He learns to feel guilt.

If a child lives with discipline – He learns self-control.
If a child lives with tolerance – He learns to be patient.
If a child lives with encouragement – He learns confidence.

If a child lives with praise – He learns to appreciate.
If a child lives with fairness – He learns justice.
If a child lives with security – He learns to have faith.
If a child lives with approval – He learns to like
himself.

If a child lives with acceptance and friendship – He
learns to find true love.

Chapter 14

Building a Healthy Family

What makes the difference between a house and a home? Is it the standard of decorating and furnishings? Or perhaps, how many mod-cons it contains? No, the answer simply is love. A house can be filled with beautiful furniture, and equipped with the latest appliances, and yet still it remains a shell. Then you can go to the poorest house with very little materially and yet be overwhelmed by the love that fills the place, and you feel 'at home'. The home of a family is a place where people know they are loved, and where they can experience acceptance. A home is place to enjoy intimacy, true fellowship and belonging.

As you read those words you may feel a little uncomfortable. Our society is far better at producing isolation and strangers than it is producing closeness and real friendship. It is an odd thing, but in our culture people talk a lot about sex and yet feel uneasy being intimate; loneliness is one of the diseases most prevalent today. As Christians we must be careful that we are not bound by the way society thinks. Life in the kingdom of darkness is different from life in the Kingdom of God. I refuse to let the world tell me how to relate to my children.

Affectionate Families

One important issue we need to settle before God is how we show our children we love them. Fathers especially, need to find a freedom in God to express both affection and love to their sons and daughters. It is an important thing for us to be able to cuddle our daughters; to develop in them an understanding of the security and affection that are produced by that contact. Today there is a great fear of children being sexually abused, and we need to be aware of the pressures that are on men in this area. Fathers, if you cuddle your daughter and feel any sexual arousal, find another brother you can trust and pray it through. Do not run away from it; face it, so that you can be free to love your daughter properly.

Let me explain one important fact I have discovered from many hours of tear-filled counselling sessions. If you can't teach your children what it is to show affection without it becoming sexual, they are very vulnerable. I struggle to express the sadness I have about so many young girls who can't remember the last time their dad hugged them. On the first occasion they go on a date and there is some affection shown, they find that they are unable to stop things and end up in bed with the boy. Sadly I am not exaggerating, and it is not necessary if you pay attention to these words:

PARENTS HUG YOUR CHILDREN

So many people have emotional problems because they have never had a true father–child relationship. By the time I meet them in the counselling room they are bottled up and unable to express their emotions. The reason is usually very simple: their parents were not emotionally involved with them when they were young.

I often heard Heather as she was feeding the babies say to them, 'I am going to make you all cuddly.' She started to express affection to them when they were very young, but didn't stop when they reached a certain age. As a result, all our children are emotionally whole. God's Word tells us to

> *'Be kindly affectionate to one another with brotherly love.'*
> (Romans 12:10 NKJV)

You may say, 'I can't do that,' but God's Word says that you can!

Don't be afraid to kiss your children. Six times the Bible commands us to greet each other with a holy kiss. In the Church, we have substituted God's direction to greet the brethren with a holy kiss, for a holy hug, or even just a handshake! A kiss is an intimate thing, yet many people do not want to get that close. Many make the excuse that this was an Eastern custom, but if you apply that to the rest of the Bible there will not be much left!

Tears are not negative or something to be ashamed of. The Bible tells us that God collects our tears in His bottle, (Psalm 56:8 KJV). He keeps them because they are precious to Him. We are told to *'rejoice with those who rejoice, and weep with those who weep'* (Romans 12:15). Yet there are many people who are so bound up emotionally that they cannot shed a few tears. Our children need to know that they can come and cry on our shoulder without any embarrassment. They will never outgrow the need for fatherly affection. If there is a real relationship there, they will never feel that they are 'too big' for it, even in their teens and twenties.

Fatherly Comfort

'For you know that we dealt with each of you as a father deals with his own children, encouraging, comforting and urging you to live lives worthy of God, who calls you into his kingdom and glory.' (1 Thessalonians 2:11–12)

Comforting is an area that is often left to mothers, yet look at Paul's words. Both comforting and encouraging are important roles for both parents. A child needs to know that his father's arm is always available and that he is always ready to listen to him.

Make it a daily goal to encourage and build up your children; it is not just the responsibility of church or school. Colossians 3:21 says,

'Fathers, do not provoke your children, lest they should become discouraged.' (NKJV)

Another meaning from the Greek for 'provoke' is to be negative with them. Always speak words that will build them up, never knock them down or humiliate them! Calling a child stupid, an idiot or telling them they are useless and hopeless will seriously damage a child's security. Even if you get frustrated with your children, never use language that will put them down.

It is very easy to damage your relationship with your children. Here is a brief list of things that can be a hindrance.

1. Constantly criticise everything they do.
2. Constantly be too busy. When they need you make them wait.
3. Make promises but don't bother keeping them.
4. Keep involving them in things that hold little or no interest to them.
5. Betray their confidence.
6. Be sarcastic.
7. Don't treat what they do seriously. Tease them, especially about things that are precious to them.
8. Ridicule them.
9. When they don't do what you want, threaten them.

Practice any of the items on that list for very long and you will find a wide gulf between you and your child. I don't think there are many adults who could maintain a relationship for long faced with this list, so we need to be especially careful with our children.

I have given you a very negative list; if you are guilty of any of the above, repent and change. To balance the above, here are some things you can do, everyday, to create a healthy home and whole, beautiful children.

1. **Be happy. Smile and develop an optimistic view.**
   Sometimes I wonder how some churches function when they are so full of pessimism. I'm known for starting the day with a positive statement 'It's the greatest day

148

you've ever lived.' Hallelujah, it can be if you are look-
ing for all the potential our loving Heavenly Father has
packed into it. Our children need to feel the optimism
we have for them. There are plenty of people who will
try to discourage your children; don't be one of them.

2. ***Affirm your children. Pay them compliments.***
Encourage them with praise regularly and mean what
you say! Let me say it again, make sure that you mean
every word you say when you praise them. Look for
opportunities to confirm what you feel about your children, look for those chances to praise them sponta-
neously.

3. ***Take an interest in your children's interests, talents and
ideas.***
Be interested in what they are interested in. It might be
hard work sometimes to keep up, in which case it will
stretch you, but as you determine to keep things in
common, your relationship will grow.

4. ***Be available.***
A minister friend of mine told his children 'I'm always
available for you. Whenever you need me, call me,
wherever I am. Even if I am in a meeting or service I
promise I'll come.' One day one of his daughters
decided to see if he was a man of his word. She worked
out when he would be in the middle of his sermon and
rang the church office. When a steward answered the
phone she said, 'It is urgent, I need to talk to my Dad
now.' When the steward explained he was busy she
said, 'Dad said I could call him anytime.' So the steward wrote a note and passed it to the pulpit where my
friend was preaching. He looked at it, excused himself,
asked someone to lead a chorus, and went to the
phone. When he answered all she said was, 'I wanted
to test you, to find out if you meant what you said.'

Perhaps you would feel that is a bit extreme but the
relationship between the two of them was made much
stronger that day. Her dad proved he was a man of his
word and his daughter discovered that she could trust

her dad. Today, when there are so many pressures on us taking so much time, take time. We have to make an extra effort to be there when our children need us. That doesn't mean being constantly in the house, it means keeping your ears open for when those times when they say 'Can I talk?'

Are you aware of the things that frighten your child? A recent study was done with under elevens and the researchers compared their results with a similar study twenty years ago. The five major fears of this age group in the early 1970s were:

1. Loud noises.
2. Dark rooms.
3. High places.
4. Dangerous animals.
5. Strangers.

Today we find the same age group have a very different list of fears.

1. Losing a parent through divorce.
2. Becoming a victim of burglary.
3. Being mugged.
4. Getting raped.
5. Getting cancer.

How drastically that list has changed in the last twenty years. The possibility that a child under eleven would even think about rape or mugging is something I find difficult to comprehend; it seems children are losing their 'innocence' at a very early age. The only way to deal with these fears is for us as parents to be filled with God's love, but we are faced with a difficult task.

Parenting in the 'Last Days'

'But mark this: There will be terrible times in the last days. People will be lovers of themselves, lovers of money, boastful, proud, abusive, disobedient to their parents, ungrateful, unholy, without love, unforgiving,

150

*slanderous, without self-control, brutal, not lovers of the
good, treacherous, rash, conceited, lovers of pleasure
rather than lovers of God – having a form of godliness
but denying its power. Have nothing to do with them.'*

(2 Timothy 3:1–5)

Notice that in that list is 'disobedient to parents'; it is one
of the signs that we are in the last days before Jesus' return.
The list above is a description of what the world will be like,
but it does not have to be a description of what goes on in
the life of the Church. I believe we can rightly expect and be
optimistic that our children will grow up to be godly, righteous and obedient. If you have faith, your family can be a
light in the darkness – a God-centred family will be obvious
in any community; aim to become a model of holiness, joy
and peace for your neighbours and friends.

A survey was done in a Young Offenders Correction
Centre. The following ten points are their advice to parents
on bringing up children:

1. Keep cool, don't fly off your handle, keep your lid on
    when things go wrong. Kids need to see how much
    better things turn out when people keep their tempers
    under control.
2. Don't get strung out from too much booze or too
    many pills. When we see our parents reaching for
    those crutches, we get the idea that nobody goes out
    there alone, and that it is perfectly OK to reach out for
    a bottle or a capsule when things get heavy. Remember
    children are great imitators. We lose respect for par-
    ents who tell us to behave one way while they behave
    another.
3. Bug us a little, be strict, show us who is Boss. We need
    to know we have got some strong supports under us.
    When you cave in we get scared.
4. Don't blow your class, stay on that pedestal. Don't try
    to dress, dance or talk like your kids, you embarrass us
    and you look ridiculous.

5. Light a candle, show us the way. Tell us God is not dead or sleeping or on vacation. We need to believe in something bigger and stronger than ourselves.

6. Scare the hell out of us. If you catch us stealing or being cruel, get tough, let us know why what we did was wrong. Impress upon us the importance of not repeating such behaviour.

7. When we need punishment, dish it out, but let us know that you still love us even though we have let you down. It will make us think twice before we make the same move again.

8. Call our bluff. Make it clear that you mean what you say. Don't compromise and don't be intimidated by our threats to drop out of school or leave home. Stand up to us and we will respect you. Kids don't want everything they ask for.

9. Be honest, tell us the truth no matter what and be straight about everything. We can take it. Lukewarm answers make us uneasy. We can smell uncertainty a mile away.

10. Praise us when we deserve it. If you give us kids a few compliments once in a while we will be able to accept criticism a lot easier. The bottom line is we want you to tell us like it is.

Chapter 15

Motherhood

Some years ago a young married lady came to me very concerned that she had become pregnant. She felt that she would not be able to be a good mother, because she did not enjoy children. I know that there are a number of young women who feel very much like this and I too was in a similar position before having children. But as soon as I became a mother, I discovered there was built within me a natural instinct to be a mother. I believe that God has placed this ability in all women, but some of us don't discover it until we actually become mothers.

God is not a bad architect. When He created us He placed within each of us all the abilities to be whatever He planned for us. In Genesis we read that God made man, male and female, and that He made both of them in His own image. Even though we have different characteristics as men and women, we are still both made in God's image. Therefore as women, there are parts of God's character that will be manifest in our lives.

Part of the Godhead is the Holy Spirit, who is called the Comforter, or in some translations the Counsellor.

> *'And I will pray the Father, and he shall give you another Comforter, that he may abide with you for ever.'*
> (John 14:16 KJV)

153

> *'But the Comforter, which is the Holy Ghost, whom the Father will send in my name, he shall teach you all things, and bring all things to your remembrance, whatsoever I have said unto you.'* (John 14:26 KJV)

> *'Nevertheless I tell you the truth; It is expedient for you that I go away: for if I go not away, the Comforter will not come unto you; but if I depart, I will send him unto you.'* (John 16:7 KJV)

I believe that this part of the Godhead is what is most commonly expressed within mothers. Comfort and the listening ear of counsel come very easily to them.

> *'Can a woman forget her sucking child, that she should not have compassion on the son of her womb? yea, they may forget, yet will I not forget thee.'*
> (Isaiah 49:15 KJV)

This verse I believe is the heart of God for what He has placed within women, but unfortunately the devil has robbed many women of this instinct. In today's society we find mothers who forget, and even abuse their children. When we become mothers we can believe that this godly instinct will be enhanced in our lives.

> *'... because the love of God is shed abroad in our hearts by the Holy Ghost which is given unto us.'*
> (Romans 5:5 KJV)

God has given us the ability to love our children even when we disapprove of their behaviour and when they are naughty and rebellious. God loved us when we were sinners, rebellious to Him, and without His love in our lives; therefore we can believe for the Holy Spirit to help us love our children. In the Bible there are several passages that tell us that God's arms are stretched out towards us to hold us up, to help and comfort us, and many others things. In other words God wishes to show us His affection, care and love. God has an attitude of affection towards us as His children. In the same way we can demonstrate our love, care, and comfort to our children because we are made in the image of God.

> *'And did not he make one? Yet had he the residue of the spirit. And wherefore one? That he might seek a godly seed. Therefore take heed to your spirit, and let none deal treacherously against the wife of his youth.'*
>
> (Malachi 2:15 KJV)

One thing which God desires from us, not just as mothers but as parents is *godly* offspring. One of the reasons why God joined us together as husband and wife was in order for us to be one flesh and produce children. Not just offspring, but godly offspring – this is part of God's will for you. In the generations before ours it was taken for granted that parents would need to sacrifice for the sake of their children who were looked upon as cherished possessions. Today, unfortunately, many parents only see their children as hindrances to their own desires for self-fulfilment. Too many parents, even in the Church, resent having to make sacrifices for the sake of their children. When we really value our children as God's gifts, sacrificing for them will not seem such hardship, but rather a privilege.

To enter motherhood with the attitude that it is the will of God, will mean the sacrifices which we all face will not seem so great to you, when compared with the blessing you will receive from both your children and from God.

Biblical Mothers

> *'Train up a child in the way he should go: and when he is old, he will not depart from it.'* (Proverbs 22:6)

When we obey God's Word and bring up our children

according to it, then we can believe that what He says will happen. Even if our children do go astray for a while, we can stand firm upon God's Word and believe that what He has promised He is well able to bring to pass. Because our experience, or the experiences of others, do not match what God's Word says, it does not nullify the Word. We must seek to make God's Word our experience by doing all we can, and then trusting Him.

Solomon became the wisest man who ever lived and he had a godly mother. Absalom, who led the nation in a rebellion against his own father had a pagan mother! Let this be an example to us and let us seek to be godly mothers who will rear godly offspring to the glory of God.

In Judges, chapter 13 we are told the story of Manoah and his wife. An angel appears to his wife and tells her they are going to have a baby boy and gives her instructions on how to behave. She is a little uncertain of herself and asks that the angel comes back and instructs them how to bring up the child. The angel does come back, but his only instruction is that the woman must be careful to do all that he had previously said; no more than that. The impression we get is that if Manoah's wife is careful to play her part right, then the child Samson would grow up correctly. What a responsibility! If we as mothers do our part, obeying God's word for our lives and for bringing up our children, then we can trust God that our children will be godly offspring.

There is another point in the life of Samson I would like to draw out at this point. When Samson saw a woman he loved, he asked his parents to go and get her to be his wife, which they did. Later in Judges 16:1 he sees a prostitute and spends the night with her. My observation is this – How often do you give in to your childrens' whims and fancies? Would Samson's life have been different if his parents had not given into his first lustful desire? We are not told that Samson had to live a single life, but he was led away by his lustful desires to the point that he lost his anointing from

God. It made him weak, and he was distracted from his life of dedication to God.

In bringing our children up one of the important things we must teach them is not to allow their selfish desires to side-track them and lead them astray from their goals in life. Sometimes, saying no to our children when they ask for things is a good discipline for them. Not always giving them all they desire will teach them self-control. It is not easy to say no, especially with all the advertising our children see on TV, and in comics and newspapers, but the truth is that if we constantly give them everything they want they will easily get into debt when they start work, running up credit card debts, and bank overdrafts. Our job is to teach them how to live without what they see and desire.

> '"As surely as you live, my lord, I am the woman who stood here beside you praying to the LORD. I prayed for this child, and the LORD has granted me what I asked of him. So now I give him to the LORD. For his whole life he shall be given over to the LORD." And he worshipped the LORD there.' (1 Samuel 1:26–28)

In giving Samuel to the Lord, Hannah brought the blessing of God upon her household. God gave her the desire of her heart and she then gave it back to God. Hannah did not consider Samuel as her's to keep. As a result she had more children. In a similar way we need to give our children back to God, who has given them to us. We who have children ought to be thankful to God that we do, because there are many women who cannot bear children of their own.

One day when we stand before God I believe we will give an account to God for the way we have brought our children up. Seeing our children as gifts which God has given us to look after for Him will help us in our attitudes towards them. God does not give us gifts to get us out of His will! God only knows how to give good gifts; therefore our children should not be seen as 'brats' or 'monkeys' sent to test us or to impede our lives.

Motherhood Brings Responsibilities

'But Mary treasured up all these things and pondered them in her heart.'   (Luke 2:19)

When we hear God speak to us about our children we must value that word. I often wonder how many times Mary talked to God about the things she treasured. When things were not going just the right way, when Jesus was growing up, when He began His ministry, when He went off to the wilderness and was tempted, did Mary go back to those words the shepherds, wise men and angel had said?

As mothers we have a responsibility to seek God for our children when they are young. Ask God for a word which will help you bring them up, to help you steer them in the right direction of God's will for them. Such a word from God can be used to live by. Believe that what God has said He will perform. I have had words from God about my family which I am still hiding in my heart and I know that one day they will all be fulfilled.

Don and I have promises for our children given when they were dedicated; for one of the boys even the age was given when God would begin to bring about the words He had given. Today that word has been fulfilled and we are seeing the promise of God being brought to completion. There was a time in our son's life as a teenager that we felt the time was right to share the word with him so that he could take on himself the responsibility of the word. He was then able to make his own decisions before God in the light of what he knew.

As mothers we need to encourage our children to take responsibility for their own walk with God and not tell them what to do all the time. In 2 Timothy 1:5 Paul says to Timothy

'I have been reminded of your sincere faith, which first lived in your grandmother Lois and in your mother Eunice and, I am persuaded, now lives in you also.'

Both of these women must have made a lasting impression upon young Timothy for him to have followed in their footsteps. I find it interesting that his father and grandfather are not mentioned. There may have been reasons why, but it is significant for us that we take this responsibility to teach the word of God to our children. That means not only the written Word but also teaching them by our example of faith and dedication, commitment and faithfulness to God.

> *'How from infancy you have known the holy Scriptures, which are able to make you wise for salvation through faith in Christ Jesus.'* (2 Timothy 3:15)

When does infancy begin? At the time of birth. I believe as mothers we must teach the scriptures to our children and not leave it to the Sunday School, or Junior Church. It is a responsibility we must take upon ourselves. Recently while reading a book I was impressed by the comments of one of the USA Senate chaplains who said that again and again he hears leaders talking about the influence of their mothers, more than they talk about the influence of their fathers! He made the observation that he felt this was because of the intimate relationship which develops during the nine months of gestation within the mother. He believes there is no way that a father can have that same kind of relationship. Although the father has the responsibility of instructing his children in his faith, most mothers probably do a better job because of the relationship they develop so early with their children.

What a responsibility! If we do desire to bring up godly offspring we must make it our goal to teach our children the word of God and all we can about our faith in God. One way for us to do this is to allow our children to see where our faith is in the practical issues of life. I remember two very clear incidents which happened with our children that I feel taught them, at an early age, that God is interested in our lives if we will give Him the chance.

One day one of our sons, who at the time was in Junior School came home quite upset because a boy at school was always picking fights with him in the playground. Next morning before going to school I asked him if we could pray about it together. He said yes, so we prayed. When he came home from school my first question was, 'What happened?' His reply was that the boy had not come near him and for the rest of his school life (and they were in the same class throughout their entire school years) he never again tried to pick a fight with our son.

The other incident concerned another of our sons, who was in infant school at the time. Don and I have lived entirely by faith throughout our ministry, and have not received a regular salary but trusted God to supply our needs, often on a daily basis. Don was away on the mission field at this particular time and money was very limited. Our son asked for some bananas before he went to school but we didn't have any and I had no money to go and buy some. I told him that we would have to believe God to send Mummy some pennies while he was at school and then I would get some for him by the time he came home. We prayed and he went off to school quite happily. First question when I picked him up later was 'Have you got some bananas?' God had been very gracious and that morning through the post I had received a gift. I told him 'Yes, God has provided some pennies' and I had been able to get some bananas. This son was, and still is, a deep thinker. He was quiet for a while and then said 'Mummy, how did God send the pennies? Did he open the sky and throw them down?' I believe this expressed his faith that God could do that if that was the way He wanted to supply for us. Still to this day, now that he is married, he has a very straight-forward trust, knowing that God loves him and will supply for him and his wife when things are not quite what they would like them to be.

'Children's children are a crown to the aged, and parents are the pride of their children.' (Proverbs 17:6)

Are your children proud of you as their parents? There is nothing worse for a child than to have parents they are ashamed of. Often through the years of our ministry Don and I have counselled young people who have been ashamed of their parents because of who they are, what they are and how they are. It has caused them a lot of heart-ache. As Christian parents we ought to seek God not just to have children that we are proud of, but also to become parents that our children can look up to and be pleased to be their parents.

There may be times when we feel discouraged by our children's reaction to God, Church, or our encouragement to live a 'clean' life. These are the times when our relationship with God will count. It will either sustain us, especially when we trust in a God who keeps His promises, or if our relationship with God is not what it should be, then we can often try to do things our way and this will end in disaster. God has given us children and He knows how to bring them up. Therefore we should involve Him in our relationship with our children. Don and I pray daily for our children, even now that they are married and have their own families. Bringing God into our family will mean we are not on our own, perhaps 'beating our heads against a brick wall'; we have Someone who is interested in us and our children. When we are discouraged, we can counteract the effects of that discouragement by keeping our eyes upon God and not the circumstances. We can replace our impatience over our children's wilful rebellion and disobedience by fixing our eyes upon Him and having an absolute assurance that God has them in His hands. This may mean a costly price for us in disciplined prayer and letting the Lord change us. At times it may be easier to just throw our hands up in utter defeat than to be disciplined in prayer and intercession on their behalf!

One area which as mothers we need to watch is after the birth of our first child. It is so easy for us to feel so fulfilled with being a mother, that we quickly neglect our husbands. 'Baby' fills our waking moments and seems to keep us occupied all day with changing, bathing, feeding, and washing. We begin to neglect ourselves and our husbands. He takes second place, and it is easy to forget that without him we would not have become a mother. This wonderful feeling of fulfilment would not have been ours without him. We must remember that we were first a wife before we were a mother and we must not neglect our husbands; if we do, this is one of the quickest ways to lose him. Many marriages have floundered at the birth of a child. Making excuses will not compensate for the rejection so easily felt by our husbands. One way to avoid this is by making an effort to communicate together, keeping our hearts open to each other, as the Bible says in James 1:19-20:

> *'My dear brothers, take note of this: Everyone should be quick to listen, slow to speak and slow to become angry, for man's anger does not bring about the righteous life that God desires.'*

Mothers can often find difficulty in maintaining a meaningful devotional time with God. The way I dealt with this was by seeing that sometimes the burdens we lay upon ourselves are not necessarily from God. I read of nowhere in the Bible that commands us to pray, or read our Bibles for a certain amount of time each day, at a specific time each day. We do have examples of people who laid such a burden upon themselves but there is not a direct command from God for us to do so. I do believe there is a lifestyle of devotion taught which we can adopt. This means having a real relationship with God that we can commune with Him at anytime, anywhere, and in whatever way we wish, be it prayer, Bible reading, Bible study, praise, singing or just direct appreciation of God and His creation. I know that some of my most precious times communing with God have been driving home after dropping children at school. We must not neglect our communion with God; it may change, but we must be diligent to ensure that it is maintained. We will be unable to raise godly offspring if we do not maintain a good relationship ourselves with God. Don't take on guilt and condemnation from others who say that we must have our 'quiet time' each day in a certain way because that will only take us further away from God. Some of the times I remember receiving from God, as my children were growing up, were when I was reading them Bible stories. I looked to God to show me new things from the stories I read which were so familiar to me.

Live in faith that God will help you to be the best mother possible to your children; then you will have the joy of being a partaker of the promise given in Proverbs 31:28:

> *'Her children arise and call her blessed; her husband also, and he praises her.'*

Chapter 16

The Joy of Discipline

If our children are brought up according to the 'Maker's Instructions' we will give them the best possible start in life. As parents we have a great opportunity to encourage them to live a life full of *'love and good works'* (Hebrews 10:24). Whatever their abilities, you as a parent have an important role as Encourager to your children. Believe the very best for them, and help them aim to achieve the best of their ability in everything.

Never, never, a million times never, tell your children that they are failures or hopeless. This can cause deep hurts that only come out years later, as we frequently find when counselling adults. Tell your children that, with God's help, they are going to make an impact in life and keep believing with them for that goal.

> *'Fathers, do not exasperate your children; instead, bring them up in the training and instruction of the Lord.'*
>
> (Ephesians 6:4)

Paul tells fathers not to exasperate their children, or as the New King James Version puts it, *'do not provoke your children to wrath.'* One way to do that is by being unreasonable. When a parent forbids their child to do a certain thing, inevitably they will be asked 'Why?' 'Because I said so, don't argue.' Does that sound familiar? Responding in this way will frustrate your child, which is a type of anger. When you do have to say no, take time to teach your children the reasons for your decisions. You will gain your children's respect by doing this.

The Dreaded Word – Discipline

In our western society discipline is a controversial subject and in some schools, almost non-existent. As you are no doubt aware, there have been concerted efforts to legally ban spanking and to accuse parents who do of abusing their children. I am convinced that God's way is the best way. In this chapter I want to set out the understanding Heather and I have reached on this important subject. What we have to share, we have lived out in our family but the basis of all we say is the Bible, the 'Maker's Instructions'.

I would add a word of caution here. If you put into practice everything we teach in this chapter, your children will soon discover that they are different. Their school companions will behave very differently and that will cause them to ask questions. You need to be able to explain to them why our attitudes and standards are different. Take time to teach them the principles you have found in God's Word.

For many parents discipline is difficult. Pressures are coming against parents from all sorts of sources, and it is easy to feel guilty that you are doing it wrong. We have a marvellous opportunity to present the Gospel in the way in which our children live disciplined lives. The world will notice the difference in them and have to admit that it works.

One of the reasons why our society is breaking down, is because parents are failing to teach their children how to live in a disciplined way. Some psychiatrists have told us that if we spank and discipline our children, we are going to make them violent. As you will see, this is totally unscriptural and actually produces the reverse effect. The explosion of violence and violent crime we read about every day is because delinquent parents have produced delinquent children; parents have failed to care for and train their children properly. If you want to know what you are like, look at your children.

A home without discipline will be a chaotic home. Our son, Stephen, when he was 16 years old, said at one of our family services, 'I am glad that both my parents discipline me. Boys at school boast that their parents have failed to discipline them. I can already see the mess that their lives are in.'

I stay in many Christian homes where the children are in charge! They have learnt to manipulate their parents, which to me is disgraceful. God has given parents a distinct role and authority in the home and they should use it.

> *'He who spares the rod hates his son, but he who loves him is careful to discipline him.'*   (Proverbs 13:24)

It is now a popular idea that by not using the rod (corporal punishment), you are loving your child. God says if you don't discipline them, you hate them! You will only see the results of how you bring up your children when they become adults, but by then it will be too late if you have done it wrong. Therefore, it makes sense to rely on God's word as a guide to bringing up our children; it has been proved to be reliable and the only 'parenting guide' that is 100% dependable.

Why do we have to use a 'rod'? I believe our hands should be a representation of our love for our children. Touch should be an expression of our care, so if we use our hands as a regular means of correction, you may cause confusion. There were occasions when I had to use my hand on my children because there was no 'rod' available. However, as a general practice I tried to use something else.

> *'Folly is bound up in the heart of a child, but the rod of discipline will drive it far from him.'*   (Proverbs 22:15)

You don't have to see many children today to discover the truth of this proverb. Sadly, many children's hearts are full of foolishness because they have not been punished. We need to make sure that we discipline for the right motives, according to the 'Maker's Instructions'.

> *'Chasten thy son while there is hope, and let not thy soul spare for his crying.'*   (Proverbs 19:18 KJV)

A father and mother need to be strong and not moved by the tears of their children. Tears can be used to manipulate, so do not allow them to influence you.

> *'Do not withhold discipline from a child; if you punish him with the rod, he will not die.'*   (Proverbs 23:13)

Discipline does not just affect the physical body, it also has spiritual consequences. If a child grows up constantly getting his own way with his parents, he will expect God to act in the same way.

> *'Punish him with the rod and save his soul from death.'*
> (Proverbs 23:14)

When you teach your child obedience, you are teaching him to obey God.

I have five children, all of whom love the Lord and are serving Him in some capacity. They all went through the so-called 'difficult' teenage years. I do not pretend that they did not have any problems, but each of them came through it well. That was because of what we put into them in their formative years.

> *'The rod of correction imparts wisdom, but a child left to himself disgraces his mother.'*   (Proverbs 29:15)

Today, child abuse is a terrible curse on our society. It is often the result of parents having no self-control. The well-publicised cases of physical abuse have added fuel to the arguments against the discipline I believe the Bible teaches. That does not mean that we should change or be embarrassed by what the Bible says; we should make sure we learn God's way and put it into practice, completely.

Discipline can go wrong and become abuse when we react and act in anger. When you discipline your child, do it calmly and carefully, with a clear reason for the punishment, and always follow it with love and forgiveness. The action that prompted 'the rod' should then be forgotten and not brought up again. If you need to, send your child to another room to give you time for any anger to abate. Never correct when you are angry, because you should always seek to show your child love and acceptance. Correcting them when you are angry can confuse that message.

Correction, according to 'The Maker's Instructions' is a hallmark of love:

> *'My son, do not make light of the Lord's discipline, and do not lose heart when he rebukes you, because the Lord disciplines those he loves, and he punishes everyone he accepts as a son.'*　　　　　　　　　(Hebrews 12:5–6)

I think it hurts me more than it hurts my children when I have to discipline them, but soon after we cuddle and make up. I have always found that my children loved me more after discipline than they did before.

God's Way Works

> *'When the wicked thrive, so does sin, but the righteous will see their downfall. Discipline your son, and he will give you peace; he will bring delight to your soul.'*
> 　　　　　　　　　　　　　　　(Proverbs 29:16–17)

The child that is disciplined will be a delight to his parents.

Some parents threaten their children with the words 'If you do that again I will smack you.' They then fail to carry out the punishment. This teaches the child to lie. If you warn your child, but don't carry it through, be careful. You risk teaching your child to never believe what you or anyone else says, including God. You must always carry out a warning – whatever the cost. Children will often push to see how far they can go and if you will keep your word. If you continue to threaten your child, but don't do what you have said you will do, they will begin to lose respect for you. The result is that it will be increasingly harder to keep discipline.

> *'He who spares his rod hates his son, but he who loves him disciplines him promptly.'*   (Proverbs 13:24 NKJV)

Note that last word – promptly. A lack of 'instant' discipline will result in a nervous child. When children test their boundaries, they do it as part of their discovery of what makes them secure. If they do something wrong but don't get punished they become uncertain. Mothers must therefore be prepared to discipline their children when they have done wrong. Don't repeatedly threaten the child with, 'wait until your father comes home.' This will make the child nervous of what punishment awaits them. It can also create a wrong relationship between them and their father, based on fear.

Be careful that you don't teach your children how to bribe. Statements like 'Mummy will give you an ice-cream if you do so and so' are not good, nor do they build a godly, serving attitude. Children need to learn to respond out of obedience to their parents, without any ulterior motives.

It is very, very important that parents never disagree about discipline in front of their children. That probably causes more harm than anything else a parent can ever do. If they watch you argue you will teach them, among other things, how to manipulate and 'play' one parent off against the other. I believe that every home needs clearly defined rules about when and what discipline will be given. Correction will always happen whenever these boundaries are crossed.

When to Stop

The responsibility to discipline your children stops only when they get married or leave home. Every child has to obey their parents until then. Contrary to popular belief and practice, the Bible says nothing about the age of consent and a change at eighteen or twenty-one. While they live in your house, everyone comes under your authority and therefore under your discipline.

Of course, you have to exercise wisdom as children get older. A young person who is fifteen years old must be treated differently from a five year old child. As your child matures, give them greater freedom, but still make sure that clear boundaries are maintained.

One boundary rule in our household has been that all our children were to be home by 10.00 pm every night. When our oldest son, Nigel, was sixteen he had a motorbike. We learnt to tell the time by listening for the bike to come up the road at 9.59 pm. He would never be late unless there was a good reason, in which case he would telephone to say what had happened. We had established the punishment for breaking this boundary and he knew it. There were times when I extended the time limit, but only after sitting down with them to find out exactly what they were going to do, where they were and the exact time we would expect them home. Apart from making sure that your children are safe, it is irresponsible to let your children come in at whatever time they like; most importantly it is your job to make sure they are ready and awake for school.

> *'For this reason a man will leave his father and mother and be united to his wife, and the two will become one flesh.'* (Ephesians 5:31)

When your children get married, let them go. On the eve of the wedding, we told each of our children 'from tomorrow, we are not responsible for you. You are no longer under our authority. But, under God's covering you are a new family unit. We will not interfere in your life and your marriage. We won't poke our noses into your affairs, but we want you to know that if you ever need help, we are here. If we can give advice we will, but only when you ask for it.'

Chapter 17

Troublesome Teenagers?

When children enter their teenage years, they go through a time when they want to experience things for themselves. Until then, even if their relationship with the Lord has been very real, it has been greatly influenced by their parents. There comes a time when they have to prove God for themselves. This may manifest in several ways, but for children who have grown up in Christian families it usually includes a bit of 'flirting' with the world. It is a time when parents need to be very prayerful and sensitive to God. They need to be very careful how they handle and respond to their children. It is important that they do not despair, but stay in faith and walk through it with God.

One of my children, had a tough time in his mid-teens. God spoke to me and said that I should sacrifice everything else and give my spare time at home to my son. I was even prepared to change events booked in my diary to make time for him. The thing he really needed was friendship with his Dad. I avoided preaching at him or constantly talking about my faith. We just enjoyed life together; so we went tenpin bowling, played billiards and visited people together. I took an interest in the music he enjoyed, and did not condemn it without knowing what it was about. We listened to it together, and although I told him when I thought something was evil, I did learn to enjoy some of it myself. When he began to learn to drive on his seventeenth birthday, Heather and I spent quite a lot of time practising with him. In quite a short period he changed. God spoke to me and in obedience to Him I responded; the result was a relationship with my son that has got better and better.

As parents we need to become friends of our children. That may sound odd, but particularly as our children discover the world around them, they need a secure 'base'. We can help them discover the world by sharing their excitement and by being prepared to talk (not preach) and listen.

Before I met Jesus, I was a football fanatic; my love of sport was really idolatry. When I was saved I repented, and for many years I did not go near a football match. One Boxing Day morning I was shaving when God spoke to me, very clearly and said, 'Take Nigel to the football today.' I was shocked, but recognised the voice of God, and so did what I was told. That afternoon really did something for our relationship.

Training

> *'Train a child in the way he should go, and when he is old he will not turn from it.'*   (Proverbs 22:6)

This is a command with a promise. If you are prepared to invest in your child and teach them correctly, God's Word says that it will last until they have grown old.

This does not apply only to training them in spiritual things. We need to train our children how to be responsible citizens; to behave properly at school; to respect teachers and those in authority over them. With so much unemployment we need to train them how to be good workers. What we put into them will help them find worthwhile employment, and produce high quality work, being their best for God in all that they do (see Ephesians 6:7).

God has made you stewards of your children. It is important to discover and develop the qualities and gifts that He has put in them. Do not try to make them come out identically. God has made everyone unique, so teach and train them to be themselves. It is also important that you do not try to make them become something you wanted to be but never did. Imposing your unfulfilled dreams and ambitions on them can be disastrous. Encourage the special and unique gifts that are in your child and treat them as 'one-offs'.

Decisions, Decisions, Decisions

A crucial part of your training is to teach your children how to make good decisions. If you continually decide for them, they will never learn how to discern right from wrong. I can remember several occasions when one of my children came to me and said, 'Dad, can I . . . ?' I told them to 'Go away and ask the Lord, and then tell me what He says.' I was not relinquishing my authority because I was always able to talk things through with them if I thought that they had made a wrong decision. However, I would not do that unless I really had to, as I wanted my children to learn that I trusted them to hear God for themselves. The ability to make decisions and then to take responsibility for the consequences, is a skill sadly lacking in our society. As parents we have the responsibility to teach them this skill, and if we do we will be equipping our children to be high quality leaders.

TV Times

The television can be a real enemy in training children. Often it is used as an 'electronic baby-sitter'. This is both dangerous and unhealthy. Television is shaping the thoughts and attitudes of children's lives more than the life-style of their parents. What a child takes into its mind in those early formative years is very, very important. Even 'Children's TV' is now filled with so much violence, filth, the occult and immoral practices, which will inevitably produce a sad harvest as those children become adults. I believe that parents should be very strict censors of the programmes children watch. Learn to use the 'OFF' switch. On a regular basis you should sit down and watch programmes with your children. If something you see is wrong, or disturbs you, talk about it, and use it as an aid to teach your children how to make right choices.

Preparing for the Future

I once stayed in the home of a Christian family where the teenage girl had her fiancé staying for the weekend. She wanted to cook him breakfast, so she asked him what he would like. He said that he would like a boiled egg. So she got a saucepan and put the egg in. One and a half hours later, she asked her father if he thought the egg was ready yet! This is not a fictional story, it actually happened. I looked at the girl and felt sad for her, but also for her parents who had really failed her.

We need to train our children to be good husbands or wives. Teach them how to handle their finances, how to live within their means. Hire purchase and credit card debts are a great curse in our society, so teach your family how to avoid getting tied up in that type of debt. Sadly, I counsel many couples whose marriage has broken down through the strain of not having enough money to finance loans and credit cards. Parents, I am appealing to you. Do something now, so that I or another church leader, don't have to spend time picking up the pieces of your child's broken marriage. Teach them how to shop around and be good stewards of what they have; develop in them the self-control to say no to the adverts they see.

There are many responsibilities around the home you can use to train your children:
- Emptying the rubbish bins;
- Setting the table;
- Washing or drying up after meals;
- General cleaning, especially of rooms they use, like their bedrooms;

 – Cleaning the car;
 – Watering the garden;
 – Keeping the garage tidy.

Sharing jobs and responsibilities will bring a sense of belonging and will help build godly principles into your children. Teach them not just by words but by sharing jobs with them. It is easy, especially with younger children, to get frustrated and say, 'I can do it quicker myself.' This does not help them.

Encouraging your child to do things is an important part of their training, even if it means putting things right after they have finished! No child is too young to start participating in family life. After they have done a job, seek to encourage them.

Fathers, train your sons how to do practical jobs around the home. Even if you aren't particularly gifted in DIY, you can teach your children how to take care of the home. If you have a garden, teach them to make use of it; it can be a lovely environment for family fun.

Mothers, teach your daughters how to be good cooks, how to sew, knit and mend, to make and take care of their clothes. Teach them how to clean and care for the home. In these days when so many mothers have to work as well, you need to prepare your daughters to cope with the pressures that this will bring.

Parents, cultivate in your children an attitude of service; teach them to be willing to sacrifice their personal preferences to serve the family. It will be hard work, and the children will moan and complain now, but they will thank you later for the skills you give them today.

Teach your children to be positive and not to allow negative thoughts to fill their minds. This will prevent them becoming prone to depression later in life. Fill them with the positive teaching of God's Word. 'I can't' is usually an excuse for laziness. Teach them how to give, and to understand that society does not owe them a living. We need to teach our children to give, and not just money, from an early age so that they grow up to be generous people.

Our children were taught to tithe from a young age; if they were given some money we encouraged them to tithe it to the church. It helped us to teach them their responsibility to church and that everything we have is God's and that we are only stewards.

I'm Not Your Mum!

There are a lot of homes where you hear the husband calling his wife 'Mum' or 'Mother'. I have been told that they are doing it for the children's sake, but it is not right. It creates a wrong image; usually I suspect that there is more to it than that. When I hear someone calling their spouse 'mother' or 'father' challenge them why they do it. Often there is a past hurt that causes them to regard their partner as a substitute parent.

We must see our partner as God intended them to be. Perhaps your wife did not have a good relationship with her father. Maybe he left home, or died, or was there but didn't function in the family. When she married you, she may still be looking for the 'dad she didn't have.' In the same way, some men look upon their wives as a mother figure. Those ties to the past need dealing with and the hurts healing.

Some may feel that this is a petty point, but I see it as very important. The man that God has given you is your husband. Treat him as such. The woman that God has given you is your wife. Treat her as such. You are husband and wife, so do not allow any other type of relationship to come between you. Then teach your children how to relate properly to you as parents. In those final years, while they are still in your home, show them how that relationship will change. Explain to them that as they become adults they don't need 'a mother/father figure' in the same way they did when young children. Decide to become good friends and you will find a rich reward in your later years.

Honour Where Honour is Due

We need to instil in our children an important principle:

> *'if one part is honoured, every part rejoices with it.'*
> (1 Corinthians 12:26)

Teach them to enjoy seeing others honoured, especially family members. From this teaching it is important that they learn that life is not 'fair'. In the story of the Prodigal (Luke 15:11–32) we can see two wrong attitudes. The younger son used his father; this was perhaps the more obvious sin of the two. However, the elder brother became jealous, feeling his father had treated him unfairly. In Genesis 37, Joseph's brothers reacted in the same way to their father's gift of a robe to his son.

Take time to teach these principles and it will bring joy to them and to you. Some parents, when one child has a birthday, insist on buying gifts for all the children. This does not teach them to honour others. I am not teaching that you should have favourites, which is wrong and very harmful. Each of my children are my favourites, and they know it. However, they are not self-centred, which is at the root of all jealousy.

Sorry

As your children grow into adulthood do make sure that they can apologize. Even if it takes an hour, waiting for a little one to say sorry **is** worth it. I can remember one of our children sitting in a hotel bedroom, while we were on a conference; we waited for two hours for the word 'sorry'. For both Heather and I that was not wasted time, because today, that child now an adult, has no difficulty apologizing. Time spent training our children is never wasted, but an investment in a life valuable to God. I think that the best way to teach principles like this to a child is to make sure that we practise them ourselves. If you can apologize to your children when you are wrong, they will quickly learn to do the same. All of us know there have been times when we have spoken wrongly, had a wrong attitude or passed judgement too hastily. Only pride will stop you going to one of your children, saying sorry and asking for forgiveness. Your children will respect you more because of such actions. It is a lie to think that you will go down in their opinion. The real result will be an adult who can forgive and be forgiven.

All Things New

As you have read these last two chapters on the art of parenting you may think that, 'it is too late' or 'we have never lived like this', or 'how do we change things now, our children are almost grown up?'

Any change must come out of a growth in relationships. It might be wise to meet together as a family and talk through the issues raised in these chapters. It is quite likely that some apologies will need to be made, to let repentance and forgiveness flow. Husbands, take the lead and start the thing going. Obviously, you will need to talk about what changes you need to make in the family's life. It will take time for those changes to have an effect, and it may be unwise to try to alter everything at once, but don't give up. You will inevitably get some bad reactions to start with, particularly as you work through the scriptural way to discipline. Stick with it, be committed to God's word and He will honour it and you. Be encouraged, no matter how old your children are, **it is never too late**.

Twelve Rules to Raise Delinquent Children

(from a Canadian Police pamphlet)

Rule 1

Begin in infancy by giving the child everything he wants. This is the way to make him grow up to believe the world owes him a living.

Rule 2

When he picks up bad words, laugh at him. This will make him think he is cute.

Rule 3

Never give him religious training. Wait till he is twenty-one and then let him decide for himself.

Rule 4

Never say, 'That's wrong!' It may develop a guilt complex or condition him to believe, when he is arrested for stealing, that society is against him and he is being persecuted.

Rule 5

Pick up everything he leaves lying around. Do everything for him. He will then be experienced in throwing all responsibility on to others.

Rule 6

Let him read anything he can get his hands on. Keep the house clean, but let his mind feed on garbage.

Rule 7

Quarrel frequently in the presence of your children. Then they won't be too shocked when the home breaks up later.

Rule 8

Give the child all the pocket money he wants. Why should things be as tough for him as they were for you?

Rule 9

Give him everything he wants to eat and drink. Surfeit him with sweets. Denial may lead to harmful frustration.

Rule 10

Always take his side against neighbours, teachers and policeman. They are all prejudiced against your child.

Rule 11

When he gets into real trouble, excuse yourself by saying, 'We never could do anything with him.'

Rule 12

Prepare for a life of grief. You're likely to have it.

Chapter 18

Relating to Unsaved Family Members

'For the unbelieving husband has been sanctified through his wife, and the unbelieving wife has been sanctified through her believing husband. Otherwise your children would be unclean, but as it is, they are holy ... God has called us to live in peace. How do you know, wife, whether you will save your husband? Or, how do you know, husband, whether you will save your wife?'

(1 Corinthians 7:14–16)

There are no techniques that can guarantee will win our families to the Lord. However, the 'Maker's Instructions' do contain several very important principles that we can apply to help us win them.

Stay in or Come Out?

'Each one should remain in the situation which he was in when God called him.' (1 Corinthians 7:20)

If you have members of your family who do not know Jesus as Saviour, stay where you are. Do not run away from them. The first place we should evangelize is our home. So, how do you relate to and reach your loved ones for the Lord?

Live a Godly Life

We must display what we believe by our lifestyle. If our words don't match our actions, our loved ones will soon see the difference and we will never win them.

When I first got saved, my mother and father were very angry. After I had been baptized in water they told me that I had made a fool of them and let them down. I did not let them put me off. I showed them day by day, what being a Christian really meant, and to the glory of God both of them were eventually converted and filled with the Holy Spirit. Our loved ones need to know that the Lord means everything to us. Are you prepared for them to test the reality of Christ in your life? Can they see that it really works?

> *'Live such good lives among the pagans that, though they accuse you of doing wrong, they may see your good deeds and glorify God on the day he visits us.'* (1 Peter 2:12)

Our lives are to be of such a standard that godless people will honour us. If we do righteous works, there is a day coming when they are going to glorify God for what they have seen in us. Here we can see the principle of sowing and reaping,

> *'Do not be deceived: God cannot be mocked. A man reaps what he sows.'* (Galatians 6:7)

Don't be disheartened; if you have been sowing for a while and there is not much reaping, it will come. If as you read this chapter you feel you have been doing things wrong don't worry. You may need to repent and ask for forgiveness, but then get on with sowing good seeds. The Bible promises that if you

> *'Sow for yourselves righteousness, reap the fruit of unfailing love, and break up your unploughed ground;*

> *for it is time to seek the* LORD, *until he comes and*
> *showers righteousness on you.'* (Hosea 10:12)

God will make sure that one day, His presence will become
so real in you that the people you live among cannot deny
it. Then they will glorify God for the righteous things that
you have done.

Going back to that passage in 1 Peter, he goes on:

> *'Wives, in the same way be submissive to your husbands*
> *so that, if any of them do not believe the word, they may*
> *be won over without words by the behaviour of their*
> *wives, when they see the purity and reverence of your*
> *lives.'* (1 Peter 3:1–2)

Note that it says *'won over without words.'* It is not necessarily what you say that will win a person, but your conduct
and lifestyle. As they see how you live, they will see *'the*
Word made flesh.' Actions do speak louder than words.
Although wives are addressed in this passage, it is a sound
principle for every member of the family. If your actions do
not match your words, anything you say will be ineffective.
Often the one you are trying to reach will be hardened even
more against the Gospel.

Peter refers to *'the purity and reverence of your lives'*
(1 Peter 3:2). The New King James Version says *'your*
chaste conduct accompanied by fear.' That fear is the fear of
the Lord. Can your loved ones see the fear of God in your
life? No one will be won if you compromise what you
believe. God can never work through compromise. If you
sin in front of your family, do not try to cover it up or
make excuses. Admit you were wrong, then apologize and
ask their forgiveness. That is so contrary to the way the
world behaves that you will actually communicate your
faith very clearly.

Love the Lord Wholeheartedly

'Do not suppose that I have come to bring peace to the earth. I did not come to bring peace, but a sword. For I have come to turn "a man against his father, a daughter against her mother, a daughter-in-law against her mother-in-law – a man's enemies will be the members of his own household." Anyone who loves his father or mother more than me is not worthy of me; anyone who loves his son or daughter more than me is not worthy of me; and anyone who does not take his cross and follow me is not worthy of me. Whoever finds his life will lose it, and whoever loses his life for my sake will find it.'

(Matthew 10:34–39)

If you love anyone else more than you love Jesus, then you are going to be in trouble. But, the more you love Jesus the more you will love those close to you. It makes sense then, that the best way to love your family is by making sure that Jesus has His rightful place in your life.

Jesus told a parable about a man that gave a party. Several people were invited to it but they declined, making a variety of excuses. One answer came back, 'I have just got married, so I can't come' (Luke 14:20). That sounds quite reasonable, but the truth is that we have no excuse for saying we cannot go Christ's way. Note Jesus' words at the end of the parable,

' "I tell you, not one of those men who were invited will get a taste of my banquet." Large crowds were travelling with Jesus, and turning to them he said: "If anyone comes to me and does not hate his father and mother, his wife and children, his brothers and sisters – yes, even his own life – he cannot be my disciple. And anyone who does not carry his cross and follow me cannot be my disciple.'

(Luke 14:24–27)

I often hear people say 'I cannot get to the meeting, my

partner does not like it.' Is this **really** true? My experience is
that it is rare for a husband not to release his wife for at
least one meeting a week. A flat refusal is usually the result
of insensitivity in the past, maybe even neglect of the family
for church activities.

The overriding principle should be love of Christ above
everything else. Our love for Jesus should be so great, that
it makes our love for others look like hate. At times that
can be misunderstood, but it is what Jesus has called us to.

Our youngest child, Faith, was born about two weeks
late. I had planned a ministry trip to Japan, so that Faith
would be born and Heather settled back at home, before I
set off. With Faith arriving late, I faced a real crisis. Two
hours after she was born Heather said to me 'You are not
cancelling your trip, God wants you there. He will take care
of me. Go!' I went, both of us knowing it was right and that
it was what God wanted.

Soon after I arrived back home a woman came up to me
and said, 'I have got something against you, Mr Double. I
must get it sorted it out.' When I asked what the problem
was, she replied, 'You left your wife three days after she
had a baby and went off to Japan. That is not right.' I had
to explain to her the cost that was involved and how
Heather had encouraged me to go. To this woman, my
actions looked like hatred of my wife; what she didn't
understand was our love for the Lord that governed our
lives. This love must be above everything else and will bring
us peace in our own hearts and love for our family, even if
they don't understand.

Do Not Compromise

As your life changes, it will be a challenge to others. I once
met an inmate of Strangeways Prison in Manchester who
had recently been converted. He had just received a reply
from his wife, after writing to tell her that he had become a
Christian. He had told her how it had changed his life and
that he was looking forward to being with her again. She

had written back, 'I don't want you to change, I like you as a criminal and want you to stay that way.'

There have been occasions when people have been separated from their families 'for the Gospel's sake'. This is an issue that needs to be faced and the principle is – don't compromise. If you live in the home of a spiritualist or someone who practises black magic you may be forced to get out, for the Gospel's sake. You may live in a very immoral home, and so have to leave. The Bible is clear about this, Jesus must come first. But there is also a strong encouragement,

> *'Everyone who has left houses or brothers or sisters or father or mother or children or fields for my sake will receive a hundred times as much and will inherit eternal life.'*
> (Matthew 19:29)

> *'I tell you the truth . . . no one who has left home or wife or brothers or parents or children for the sake of the kingdom of God will fail to receive many times as much in this age and, in the age to come, eternal life.'*
> (Luke 18:29-30)

The only reason for leaving our loved ones is for His Name's sake and for His Kingdom's sake. That does not necessarily mean you must leave in the sense of physically moving away. It may be necessary, but often it means not getting involved in some family get-togethers, or events. If you know there is going to be something unrighteous or sinful happening you may have to say that you won't take part. Don't be tempted to compromise for 'a quiet life'. Jesus promised that if we are prepared to stand for Him, He would reward us. The way of compromise always loses!

Love Your Relatives

Seek to be the best wife, husband, son, daughter or parent in the world. This involves caring and having an interest in them all as people. Sadly, when one member is converted, he or she often loses interest in the rest of the family. This will drive them away from God instead of winning them. Obviously you must not be involved in anything unrighteous, but you don't have to isolate yourself from them. Some unsaved husbands I meet feel that another man has stolen their wife! This is serious; a wife may have fallen in love with Jesus, but that love should have a positive affect on the love she has for her husband, not the reverse.

Our great example is Jesus. Jesus was not religious; it was always the religious that were most offended by Him, never the 'man on the street'. Jesus was at home with tax collectors, prostitutes and sinners, though He himself remained sinless. Instead of avoiding Him, the unsaved were happy to be in His company; Jesus was not threatened by them, nor did they feel 'got at' by Him. There was something attractive and winning about Him. Levi, the tax collector, even put on a great feast in his own home for Jesus.

> *'When the teachers of the law who were Pharisees saw him eating with the "sinners" and tax collectors, they asked his disciples: "Why does he eat with tax collectors and 'sinners'?"'*
> (Mark 2:16)

> *'"For John the Baptist came neither eating bread nor drinking wine, and you say, 'He has a demon.' The Son of Man came eating and drinking, and you say, 'Here is a glutton and a drunkard, a friend of tax collectors and "sinners".'"'*
> (Luke 7:33–34)

Perhaps the most common accusation the world has against the church is that it is boring. Jesus came that we might have life, and *'have it more abundantly'* (John 10:10 NKJV). He came so that we might enjoy life to the full. Do you? When you are 'witnessing' do you have to put on a show? We need to learn to relax and simply let the life of God within us shine through.

Seek to be your loved ones' best friend. Accept them as they are; remember, that is how Christ accepted you. Too often believers expect Christian behaviour from their non-Christian relatives. This is an unfair expectation. We need to remember that anything good in our lives is the result of God's work in us. Don't complain, but be grateful for any good points they may have! We must accept them as they are, and believe for change, for love has an amazing transforming effect.

Do Not Preach at Them

This is one sure way of driving your relatives away. I heard of one wife who tried to win her husband by 'firing' Bible texts at him every time he came home. He would be sitting, eating a meal and she would preach at him from the other side of the table. Even when he went to bed at night there was a tract under his pillow!

Do not try to nag them into the Kingdom! You will never win anyone in this way. Arguing is not the way either. Wives with unsaved husbands, often ask me for advice on how to win them to the Lord. What I say is:

1. Stop preaching at him.
2. Don't arrange for other Christians to come in to 'have a word' with him.
3. Seek to be the best wife in the world to him.
4. Compliment him.
5. Cook his favourite meals for him.
6. Satisfy him sexually.
7. In short, love your husband.

Do this and it will not be long before he will wonder what has happened to you. Then you can say, 'The Lord Jesus has just put such a love in my heart for you. Wouldn't you like to get to know Him too?' But, please, make sure this is a genuine expression of your love. If he responds to the Lord that is great, but even if he doesn't, keep on loving him.

Seek to Persuade Them

Although we are not to preach to our unsaved relations, the Bible does encourage us to seek to persuade them (2 Corinthians 5:11). Believe and pray for those moments when you can gently share something about the Lord. Ask God to give you a sensitivity to Him and your loved ones. From time to time it may be appropriate to invite them to special meetings and events; be gentle, considerate and sensitive in how you do it. There was a time when our church regularly had parties. Any time someone had a birthday or anniversary in the church we would have an outreach party, and the church would invite others in. These were great evenings together, and we usually finished with a short epilogue. Several people were won to the Lord as a result. Often, relaxed, fun times break down many of the barriers non-churched people have and they are able to lose their 'religious' ideas about what being a Christian is all about.

Encourage your friends from the church to come to your home. For all sorts of reasons many Christians are shy or worried about doing this, but, it should be a very natural thing. Don't invite 'hot Gospellers' who are likely to make the family feel embarrassed. I am talking about having friends in for a cup of tea or for a meal. This can often lead to further opportunities to do things together, like playing sport or sharing in other areas of common interests. Your family needs to discover that Christians aren't 'weird' and won't condemn them if they say the wrong thing or 'put their foot in it'.

Be natural; you don't have to talk about 'spiritual' things or about subjects that will exclude your family. A deep theological debate about Sunday's sermon is not going to help. Talk about real life, because you want to communicate that Christians are normal people, but different!

Often as I travel, I am accommodated in homes where there is an unsaved partner. This is often done deliberately, as people think, 'He's an evangelist. He'll win them to the Lord.' I have won a few people to the Lord in this situation, but not in the way that was expected of me. If I stay in a home where there is an unsaved person, one of my goals is to find a point of contact, a subject we have in common.

On one occasion I was lodged in the home of a business-man who was not a believer. His wife was, and it appeared that she had persuaded him to allow 'the preacher' to stay. After being introduced, we began to chat over a cup of coffee, talking about his business and other interests in his life. Soon the conversation got around to football, so I asked him, 'Do you watch "Match of the Day"?' He replied, 'Yes, do you?' and so we agreed to watch it together that evening. Later, when I returned from the meeting, he already had the television on. I took off my shoes, put my feet up, made myself at home, and began very naturally to build a friendship. The next evening he came with us to the meeting and was saved! This type of evangelism, as with all evangelism, requires us to take a genuine interest in the person. They are not another 'scalp' but an individual that God loves and cares for, and we should have the same attitude. Unsaved people do not want to feel 'got at' or that they are a target.

Respect Them

When we try to communicate the good news to people, it is very important that we maintain an attitude of respect for them as a person God loves. If we appear 'superior', all we will communicate is that 'we know better'. That will not win them.

Another lady came to me for advice about a problem she had. She was married to a non-believer and because her problem was 'spiritual' she felt she couldn't talk to her husband about it. After she had told me what was wrong I said, 'Your husband is the head, go and ask him.' She reacted angrily, 'I can't, he's not saved.' Although I explained that the Bible doesn't say 'He's head only if he is a Christian,' she went away clearly upset. Sometime later I was back in the same church and the lady came up to me again and said,

'Mr Double, I want you to know that I was very cross with your advice. But I went home and thought about it and I did what you said. I asked my husband and he gave the answer I needed, and what is more he's been more interested in the church since then.'

Although an unsaved person has different values, we need to be careful to obey biblical principles. If we do, God will honour His word and will work things for our good.

Pray for Them

> *'The earnest (heartfelt, continued) prayer of a righteous man makes tremendous power available – dynamic in its working.'* (James 5:16 The Amplified Bible)

Pray for your family. Don't give up. Your prayers will release dynamic power, so if your partner, parent or child is going to be converted to Christ, it will only happen when the dynamic power of God is involved. Believe that as God hears your prayer He will answer. But, be careful – a great deal of prayer for the unsaved is motivated out of selfishness rather than a love for them. Are you totally convinced that without Christ they are destined for eternity separated from God? I have heard too many prayers for unsaved relatives that are really saying 'Lord, please save them because it would make my life much easier.' This is an important question to answer, why do you want your partner saved? For their benefit or yours?

If we love someone, our prayers should be continual; don't give up. It is this heartfelt, continuous prayer that brings God's power into the situation. We need to realise that our timing is often different to God's. Do not get discouraged or give up praying, but remain in faith for them. Study God's Word and discover some of His promises concerning the family:

> *'I now establish my covenant with you and with your descendants after you.'* (Genesis 9:9)

*'I will pour out my Spirit on your offspring, and my bles-
sing on your descendants ... One will say, "I belong to
the LORD"; ... another will write on his hand, "The
Lord's." '*   (Isaiah 44:3, 5)

*'Believe in the Lord Jesus, and you will be saved – you
and your household.'*   (Acts 16:31, see also
Deuteronomy 30:19 and Acts 3:25)

There is no substitute for God's Word in producing faith
in your heart. If you merely pray out of sentiment, you will
soon get frustrated and give up. It is God's Word that gives
us the strength to hold on in faith, even if there is no evidence of change. The truth is that because we are so close to
them, we are probably more able to pray for them effectively than anyone else. Be sensitive to the Lord. He can
show you how to pray about the details of their lives, and
how He can reach them.

Finally, we all need that very precious fruit of the Holy
Spirit – patience. Settle in your heart and spirit that God
wants your unsaved family in His Kingdom more than you
do. Then by living righteously, all out for the Lord, and by
taking the opportunities He gives, loving and showing an
interest in them, you will reach them and win them for
Christ.

Chapter 19

Extended Families

'God sets the lonely in families, he leads forth the prisoners with singing; but the rebellious live in a sun-scorched land.'   (Psalm 68:6)

Within every one of us there is a strong desire to belong. I have yet to meet anyone who has not got that real longing inside to know that they belong to someone or something. God made us that way. He said,

'It is not good for the man to be alone.'   (Genesis 2:18)

Most of the problems that I deal with when counselling are because, deep down, people want to belong but don't feel that they do.

A person who is rejected will always look for acceptance. I know from experience, for many years I always wanted people to belong to me. I looked for my family, for my team and for my church to be mine. When I was set free from rejection, I realized that I belonged to them.

I have prayed for many hundreds of people to be set free from this bondage to rejection and past hurts. One lesson that I have learnt is that there cannot be any permanent cure from rejection unless good relationships are established. To be in a situation where you are alone will not help you learn to relate to others.

Loneliness is one of the most common diseases on the Earth. It is a disease of the heart, because you can be in a crowd of people and still feel lonely. My definition of loneliness is; the lack of a deep relationship with anybody. Husbands and wives will be lonely if they have not got a deep relationship with each other. You can live in the same house, even sleep in the same bed and yet still be lonely because you don't have a real friendship. There are many children who are lonely because they do not have a deep relationship with their parents. Many people are lonely in the church; they will shake hands and maybe even hug you, but they have no relationships. A reason for this is that lonely people expect others to start building a relationship with them and are reluctant to make the first move. For all of us, it is our responsibility, we can't blame other people if we are lonely.

> *'By this all men will know that you are my disciples, if you love one another.'* (John 13:35)

How we need a new infusion of God's love. This will speak more loudly than any preaching or 'open airs' on street corners. It is not sufficient to say to someone 'God loves you', we need to be the love of God to them. The Bible tells us that it is hypocritical to say to someone, 'be warmed and be filled,' yet doing nothing practically about it (James 2:16).

Loneliness is painful, and causes all kinds of problems; as members of the body of Jesus we need to look for lonely people, and do something about it. If our churches work as God intended, everyone will be cared for. One way that this works is through extended families. By that phrase I mean people who are not blood relations, but are regarded as members of a particular family. (They may or may not physically live in the same house.)

God said that it is not good that man should be alone (Genesis 2:18), and that He puts the lonely (or solitary) in families (Psalm 68:6). Jesus believed this. When He was hanging on the cross,

> *'Jesus saw his mother there, and the disciple whom he loved standing nearby, he said to his mother, "Dear woman here is your son," and to the disciple, "Here is your mother." From that time on, this disciple took her into his home.'*
> (John 19:26–27)

I honestly believe that there is no better answer for today's generation of lonely people than God's idea – extended families. It is the answer to so many people who have never known the love of their parents. They can discover the joy of being part of a family where they know that they belong.

Those in my extended family have the same place in my heart as my own children. We do not treat them differently and they aren't lodgers. If any member of my family is hurt or ill, then I am emotionally affected. Why? Because God has given them to me. That is an important principle to understand. I will not take anyone into my family just out of sympathy, but only when I am certain that God has given them to me. He gave me my 'natural' children and He gave me my extended family. Only the method of receiving them was different. If God has given them, how can there be any difference in the way I treat them? (We do not like using the words 'extended family' because we are just one family.)

> *'The alien living with you must be treated as one of your native-born. Love him as yourself, for you were aliens in Egypt. I am the LORD your God.'*
> (Leviticus 19:34)

Men, in our society there is a desperate lack of fathers. Will you be one? Everyone needs a family they can relate to, where they know that they are loved and feel a part of what is happening; that still applies even if it is not possible for them to live under the same roof. The person who lives on their own in a flat, needs to relate to a family. The door needs to be open to them, so they feel welcome and part of the family. I suggest they have their own key, so that they can come and go when they want, without feeling like a visitor or intruder.

Frances was a member of our household for several years. She is now married with a family of her own. Looking back on the time she lived with us she says, 'I know that the relationships I built with the family will last for eternity. They didn't stop when I got married; they are forever. I know when I was part of the Double household that I was loved, cared for and wanted for who I was within the family.'

I believe that it is God's best that everyone should relate to a family. Do not misunderstand me and immediately take a dozen people into your home, saying, 'God said I am going to be a father to them.' Get your relationships right with your own children first, then let God add to the family one at a time. It is important to work things out with them before you take any others in. But I do want to challenge you – if God has given you a home, don't be selfish with it, share it.

Those who have come to live in our home have enriched our 'natural' children; they have not taken from them. My children could not imagine life without the precious people God has given us.

Taking the Initiative

It is very important that the whole family is involved in the decision of new people joining the family. If the parents or even the majority invite someone, without everyone's complete consent, you could find your children getting hurt, becoming resentful or feeling that they are losing out. In the past we have set aside special times as a family to pray and share together, before reaching a decision on someone new. If we are not all convinced that God is giving the person to us, then the answer must be **'No'**.

A good example was when Peter came to join the Good News Crusade team and moved down to Cornwall. Heather and I felt that it was right for him to be in our family; in practical terms there was no way that he could, because there were no spare bedrooms. When we got together as a family and talked it through, Stephen, who was 13 years old at the time, immediately said, 'He can share my room.' We felt that was an indication that it was right for Peter to join us.

Sometimes, the reason for extended family is simply geographical, for example when people move away from their parents to work or to study. There are also many people who are casualties of our society. The homeless, those who have been abused and those who have come from 'broken homes'. God may ask you to extend your family for any of these.

I do not believe that it is right that every person, when they leave their parents' home, should live in a flat; if family life has been bad and they have never experienced family relationships that work, an 'extended family' could help them a great deal. Not knowing how God intended a family should work has been the cause of many ship-wrecked marriages. Marriage is not the best situation to work out your first good relationship.

I have deliberately tried to avoid presenting this subject in a mechanical way. It is impossible to write a 'how to' guide to extending your family. Every family and every situation will be different, and you will need to work it out carefully. Some people have opened their homes under pressure or because they felt sorry for a person. Compassion is vital, but it does not make a calling. You must hear from God and know in your heart that it is right to take a person into your family.

Behind the Mask

Because people have been hurt in the past, they often wear a mask, trying to hide their real self in case they get hurt again. Before they are willing to take off their mask and tell you their innermost secrets and fears, they have to be satisfied that you really love them and can be trusted. This takes time, but it is only then that you can minister the Lord's healing to them and begin to build genuine relationships.

Taking someone new into your home can be painful; they may have been used to doing things in ways unacceptable to your family. Therefore, their first reactions to discipline may be quite stormy. On occasions we have had to meet together as a family to face certain issues. Once, we had to strongly confront a new member of the family who had sinned and not owned up to it. They came to the place where they admitted their sin, and made restitution. Immediately there was a tremendous love flowing from the family to that person. It brought more security to the individual involved because they discovered that nothing they did would change the family's commitment to them. Whatever we discover about each other should not stop us still loving and accepting.

Extending your family can be a great source of joy and enrichment for everyone involved. As Heather and I look back at the various people who have lived in our home and been a part of our family it is very rewarding to think that we have had a significant influence in their lives. I would encourage you to think very seriously about what I have said in this chapter, and ask the Lord how you should respond.

Chapter 20

Grandparents, In-laws and Other Relatives

Our aim in writing this book is to set out, in a practical way, God's order for the family. We hope that as you are reading it, you can identify areas where you can improve your marriage or family life. As you start to bring more of God's plans into your lives, we are convinced that God will bless you. In this chapter we want to look at some relationships that are often the cause of tension and bad feeling in the family. We want to talk about the role of grandparents and in-laws, and highlight the important contribution they can make to your family.

> 'For this reason a man will leave his father and mother and be united to his wife, and they will become one flesh.'
>
> (Genesis 2:24)

Before we look at individual roles, I want to make clear the process that occurs when a couple marry and form a new family unit. If this process takes place properly everything else will work, but if it doesn't, problems are bound to happen. Genesis 2:24 illustrates this process:

To leave → To cleave → One flesh

The first step to being married is for the couple to leave their families, to start a new one. They then cleave together, and become one flesh. Steps two and three of the process are dealt with elsewhere in this book; the first step is very applicable as we think about relationships with the wider family.

To Leave

Leaving should be a public act. In some parts of Africa today, when a man gets married to a lady from another village, people will dance with him as he goes from his home to her village. This is an 'echo' of the old Jewish marriage celebration. It involved the bridegroom travelling with his companions from his home to his bride's and then processing with her back to his home (cf. Matthew 25).

The marriage ceremonies of our culture don't have such a useful visual impact, but parents, the same principle still applies – when your children do marry, **let them go**. I appreciate that going to college, or moving away for work, can mean that the point at which your child 'leaves' is very unclear. Today, the traditional way may not be 'normal', but that does not change God's Word. Make the decision that when they start a new family unit, by getting married, you will let your children leave your family unit.

The truth is that it is not that hard for young ones to leave home, but it is hard for the parents to let them go. Often it can be worry that stops us: 'Is his washing going to be done properly?', 'Is she going to cook the right meals?' All these things go through our minds, and that is natural because we care; how we react is important, because it is then that we will know if we have let them go, or if we are still 'holding the strings'. God's way is – let them go.

If you get this principle established in your hearts now, you will receive a blessing. How? When your child leaves, you will not become 'in-laws'. Many jokes have been made about the 'mother-in-law' and a lot of tears shed because of interference from them. God's intention was something very different. Don and I express it in this way: we are not 'in-laws', we are 'in-loves'. The relationship you have with your child has to change when they get married. However, the love that was there before will still be there and that should be the basis of your relationship from now on.

Leaving does not mean abandoning. We have got five children, all now married; none of them have abandoned us, but they have all left. Don and I feel that they constantly care for us. It takes work to adjust, but the rewards are great. This is especially true when your children start having children of their own, and that is when we move on to the God-given role of grandparent.

To produce good grandparents you have to start the day the baby is born – which is to say not the grandchild or the child, but the grandparent. That is how long it takes to shape a grandparent!

Grandparents are a very important part of family life. If we exclude them, we leave out a significant part of the 'Maker's Instructions' and that is dangerous. Although it is obvious, it does need stating that grandparents have already been parents, so they have got something very valuable to offer experience of life. We can learn a lot from them, both mistakes and successes. Sometimes I think God must get a little frustrated when we make the same mistakes our parents did. Especially when we can easily avoid them by taking time to talk to each other. Can you learn from other people's mistakes? You don't have to go through the school of experience on everything. You only need to be sensitive and watch the mistakes of others.

To learn from our grandparents depends on a good relationship, which is true for every part of the family. Function needs to be based on relationship, not just upon a title. As I have already said in this book, there are a lot of men who are called 'father' but they do very little fathering. For them it is purely a title. To be a true father speaks of relationship, and it is the same with grandparents.

A Good Example

'I have been reminded of your sincere faith, which first lived in your grandmother Lois and in your mother Eunice and, I am persuaded, now lives in you also.'

(2 Timothy 1:5)

Grandparents will be role models for their grandchildren; they should set a godly example for the little ones to follow. When Paul saw Timothy there were three generations of sincere faith, a tremendous heritage. Paul wrote to Timothy to stir up the gift that was in him (2 Timothy 1:6) so that he reached his full potential in God. The seed of that potential went right back to his grandparents.

What example are you setting your grandchildren? One day I was in a meeting, and my grandson Joshua was at the back of the room. He was only two at the time but he was watching me. We were praising God, but out of the corner of my eye I was watching him. Every time I clapped, he clapped and when I did a little jig around and danced, he danced. If I put my hands up, he put his hands up. He watched me and copied everything I did.

It taught me a lesson – if he watched me then, he will be watching at other times, and what will he learn? If I was to get irritable with Heather in front of Joshua, he would see and could think that if Granddad can get annoyed then so can Joshua. Our example is so important and it will be a fruitful ministry.

'So that you, your children and their children after them may fear the LORD your God as long as you live by keeping all his decrees and commands that I give you, and so that you may enjoy long life.' (Deuteronomy 6:2)

I believe one of the greatest needs in our society is for children to be taught respect. I believe parents can get a lot of help from grandparents and other relations. They have a role in teaching our children the fear of the Lord, which is the basis of all respect.

The fear of the Lord is something that must be learnt.

> *'I will teach you the fear of the LORD.'*
> (Psalm 34:11, see also Psalm 86:11)

It doesn't just happen, so don't expect your children or your grandchildren to suddenly start fearing God, not even when they get born again.

One member of my team asked me to teach him the fear of the Lord. So I did it in a very simple way: I told him to get a concordance and a Bible and look up every reference to the fear of the Lord. Then in an exercise book he put three columns: one column was titled 'Fear of the Lord,' the next 'Little fear of the Lord' and in the third 'No fear of the Lord.' As he looked at the scriptures he had to apply them to his own life and then tick the column that described him. He used to come back every two or three weeks to show me how far he had got. At first nearly all the references were in the 'No' column with the odd one in 'Little.' But, as he went on studying and praying, the ticks moved over until it was almost all 'Fear' and 'Little' and no 'No's'.

> *'Only be careful, and watch yourselves closely so that you do not forget the things your eyes have seen or let them slip from your heart as long as you live. Teach them to your children and to their children after them.'*
> (Deuteronomy 4:9)

You must be diligent about obeying God's laws yourself and make sure they are in your own life. Remember that you can never have a day off from serving God, or fearing Him, or walking in the light of the Lord, because every day you are being watched. Your grandchildren will see how you live before God. So it is by your lifestyle and example that your grandchildren will be convinced of your faith.

But, it must always be built on good relationships. Your ability to be good grandparents can only be built on the good relationship you have with your children. Be warned, if you don't have that, you will be called interfering and your motives will be questioned.

> *'Even while these people were worshipping the LORD, they were serving their idols. To this day their children and grandchildren continue to do as their fathers did.'*
> (2 Kings 17:41)

We have looked at the blessings of a good example but let's note how dangerous the bad example is. I don't want to comment on the issue of smoking here, but it provides a good illustration of this point. I have met several 'secret' smokers as I stay in different people's homes. I have got a very good sense of smell and that kind of secret does not stay a secret very long! The point is, they may say that they smoke 'secretly', yet before long you start smelling it on their children. The parent teaches their child, who then teaches their child, and to misquote scripture, 'what is done in secret won't be shouted from the housetops, but will be smelt by those with a good sense of smell!' I believe there is a path we follow – what the grandparents do, there is a good chance that their children and then their grand-children will do it too.

Another illustration of this point is the way many fathers are guilty of leading their sons into the bondage of free-masonry. This may go from one generation to the next and can cause immense spiritual problems. Again, what example are you giving if your grandchildren see you reading the horoscopes? Don't say, 'I don't believe them', because your words and your actions won't match.

Heather and I have spent many hours helping young people deal with problems caused by parents and grand-parents involved in spiritism, freemasonry and similar activities. These things do come down the hereditary line, and although it might not be deep involvement something is imparted. Our counselling often involves deliverance and cutting people off from past ties. The effects of a bad example to grandchildren can seriously influence their lives.

> *'You shall live in the region of Goshen and be near me – you, your children and grandchildren, your flocks and herds, and all you have.'* (Genesis 45:10)

Here we touch a 'thorny' issue. Our society has been conditioned to think that distance isn't important, but mobility is. Contrary to popular belief the 'nuclear' family is not part of God's plan. I believe that as you read the Bible you will find that God's intention is that grandparents, parents and children should live in close proximity.

Let me challenge you. If you were offered a promotion, or a highly paid job that required you to move to the other side of the country, what would you do? I hope that you would pray to make sure it was God's plan for you. But would you be surprised if God said, 'Stay because of your family?' Would you decline the offer for the kingdom of God's sake and for your family's sake? I believe that God can take care of your job and bless you. It might take longer to get promoted, but are you willing to stand for God's order?

I believe there is a very important principle in the wider family sharing together. In some parts of Africa you can often see the reality of this: a couple have a plot of land where they have their hut, grow their food, keep their animals, and it is economic base for all they are. When each of the children get married, the parents give them a little part of their plot, to build a separate house. That is how close parents and children live to each other. Then when the grandchildren get married, they are given a plot; sometimes you can see four or five houses on a single plot with each different generation still there, in close proximity.

While economics and culture mean we can't build houses in the same way, I believe the principle is still relevant. I read of one eminent social worker who explained why they are such a busy profession: as this generation has seen the creation of the 'mobile' family, many families have moved a long way from the parental home. The effect is that those families have lost the value of a grandparent's participation and contribution.

> *'But if a widow has children or grandchildren, these should learn first of all to put their religion into practice by caring for their own family and so repaying their parents and grandparents, for this is pleasing to God.'*
>
> (1 Timothy 5:4)

After children leave home, they still have a responsibility to honour their parents. It makes me feel very sad to see the way that old people are often treated. Many children opt out of their responsibility, putting their parents in old people's homes. The truth is that there are many brokenhearted people in such places.

Our parents made great sacrifices for us as we grew up. When they are old, it is our responsibility to care for them. For instance, I tell my mother to keep warm during the winter and that I will help settle the bills. Additionally, the five grandchildren and I have agreed to make a regular standing order into her bank account; it's not very much but everyone is playing their part. It means that, along with the small pension she gets, she has enough to live on and does not have the pressure of where the next penny is coming from. You could argue that it is the Government's responsibility, but no, the Word of God is our guide. We'll get all we can out of Social Security, but we must also make sure we play our part.

I think it is a tragedy when elderly people are put into homes when it could be avoided. Sometimes they are so ill and incapacitated that it may be necessary. However, I believe that, if possible, to keep them in a family environment is by far the best.

There is a lot that the Bible says about grandparents. I have only mentioned a few of the many references and it would make a good study, particularly if you are soon to be blessed with grandchildren.

> *'Grandchildren are the crown of old men.'*
>
> (Proverbs 17:6)

Do you believe that? I am not an old man yet but I am enjoying my crown. We have seven grandchildren and are expecting more; when I am old I will have a big crown! I don't know how many stars will be in it, there are seven there now and I believe more are coming.

Uncles and Aunts

> *'Mordecai had a cousin named Hadassah, whom he had brought up because she had neither father nor mother. This girl, who was also known as Esther, was lovely in form and features, and Mordecai had taken her as his own daughter when her father and mother died.'*
>
> (Esther 2:7)

There are many cultures across the world where this is still practised. Jackson, one of the men in Tanzania whose ministry we support, has done this. His brother died and so Jackson and his wife took his brother's three children straight into their family. That example may seem a bit distant from your situation. However, there is an issue that is similar in this country. The role of uncles and aunts could have a significant effect in answering the problems of some single parents today. Often these families struggle on their own, when some pressure could be relieved by uncles and aunts and grandparents. It can also be the answer for wayward teenagers who say no-one gives them time to talk. The insecurity, hurt and pain that comes from rejection, particularly in divorce, can be answered by a committed uncle or aunt.

From my personal experience I know the benefit of uncles and aunts who took time to care. During the war my

Dad was away in the forces; I remember with great affection one of my uncles having an active role in my life. I still lived with my Mother, but he took me into his heart and cared. He was a gas fitter, which meant he often brought home off-cuts from the lead pipes. He used to make me little lead soldiers and eventually I had over 100 soldiers and a fort. More importantly I have got some very treasured memories of a man who had the patience and the kindness to show me friendship when I needed it.

Parents, open your homes to those other adults who can positively affect your children's growth and development. Let the children learn from them, don't be threatened. It does not imply that you are being a bad parent, and it is a lie to believe you have to do it on your own. As you open your home you will discover another great secret – you will get blessed as well.

PART FOUR

When Things Go Wrong

Chapter 21

The Great Divide

In a book about God's plan for marriage, why do we include a section about things going wrong? If we have set out God's ideal for us, is this necessary? By addressing the issues of divorce and remarriage, are we accepting less than God's best? Heather and I have included the next three chapters for all those couples who did not get any teaching about marriage the 'first time around'. If you have experienced the pain and tragedy of divorce, then this section is for you.

Heather and I regularly conduct weekends of teaching for married couples. On one such weekend in a Pentecostal Church, 27 couples attended. At the start of the first session I asked them to introduce themselves. After the first couple mentioned that they were in their second marriage, everybody else did the same and told us which marriage they were in. 20 of the 27 couples were in their second or third marriages; these were people who were members of the church. It really opened my eyes, and convinced me that if we want to minister the life of God and His Word effectively, we cannot ignore what is happening around us. Sadly, because of the arguments about the doctrine of divorce and remarriage, many people who have been divorced, or have married again, have felt excluded from the Church.

Heather is my second wife and at the time of writing we

have just celebrated our 30th wedding anniversary. I got married before I was saved and have two children from my previous marriage. Both Heather and I have first-hand experience, and have accumulated theory from the Word of God about this subject. However, we have still got our 'L' plates on, we are still learning, and don't want to appear to have all the answers; we have experienced God's grace and want to share with others that are in similar situations.

> *'For this reason a man will leave his father and mother*
> *and be united to his wife, and they will become one flesh.'*
> (Genesis 2:24)

From the beginning, God planned that the covenant two people make when they get married should be lifelong. It was to be an 'until death do us part' relationship. Divorce was never God's intention; we are told that God hates divorce (Malachi 2:16). It is always the result of sin and causes hurt to those involved, not least the children.

Divorce, today, is a reality and must be faced. Inside and outside the Church are many people who are either divorced or remarried. They want to know where they stand as far as God's Word is concerned.

On one side, our permissive society has offered the ultimate answer to divorce: 'Don't get married, just live together.' The Church, however, has often self-righteously gone the other way. In many churches I have visited, divorcees and those who have remarried are regarded as 'second class citizens'. Some pastors, sadly, seem to consider divorce and remarriage as the 'unforgivable sin'. I know divorcees who have been banned from preaching, holding a church office, counselling or even singing in the choir. My experience is that this has often been done with no consideration of either the causes or the biblical legitimacy of the divorce. Sadly, many Christians totally lack compassion for those who have been involved in divorce and adultery. Our attitude should be the same as that of Jesus (Philippians

2:5). He clearly showed us, through the way He responded to the woman caught in the act of adultery recorded in John 8:3–11.

Many Christians either assume that the Bible has nothing to say about divorce or think that it simply condemns it. Neither is true! In this chapter I want to consider what the Bible says, so please lay aside any personal prejudices you may hold, and come with an open heart to God's Word.

Although God hates divorce, he recognizes it and does not condemn it. Instead, He lays down some clear principles and guidelines that we need to understand. Were you aware that God himself divorced Israel?

> *'I gave faithless Israel her certificate of divorce and sent her away because of all her adulteries. Yet I saw that her unfaithful sister Judah had no fear; she also went out and committed adultery.'* (Jeremiah 3:8)

Those who say they will have nothing to do with anyone who is divorced must logically include God in their excommunication! The Bible even records 113 divorces that took place to honour God (Ezra 10:11–17).

Old Testament Law

> *'If a man marries a woman who becomes displeasing to him because he finds something indecent about her, and he writes her a certificate of divorce, gives it to her and sends her from his house, and if after she leaves his house she becomes the wife of another man, and her second husband dislikes her and writes her a certificate of divorce, gives it to her and sends her from his house, or if he dies, then her first husband, who divorced her, is not allowed to marry her again after she has been defiled. That would be detestable in the eyes of the LORD. Do not bring sin upon the land the LORD your God is giving you as an inheritance.'* (Deuteronomy 24:1–4)

In the laws God gave to Moses, an official bill of divorce could be signed, which released a partner to remarry. To avoid the adultery laws, the Hebrews had developed a way of sidestepping them. They would divorce one partner, then take another, on the grounds that if the new relationship did not work out, they could always go back to the first! God condemned these 'trial marriages'. He made it clear; if a person has remarried then it is too late for a change of mind! The divorce was final. The idea that two divorced people are 'still married in God's sight', as some have taught, is not only unscriptural but extremely harmful.

God hates divorce, but not every divorce is sinful. The Lord lays down certain legitimate reasons for divorce in His Word. Although divorce often happens because of the hardness of people's hearts, in certain situations it is permitted by God. In 1 Corinthians 7, Paul considers the subject under two sections:

The Believer with an Unbelieving Partner

'If any brother has a wife who is not a believer and she is willing to live with him, he must not divorce her. And if a woman has a husband who is not a believer and he is willing to live with her, she must not divorce him. For the unbelieving husband has been sanctified through his wife, and the unbelieving wife has been sanctified through her believing husband. Otherwise your children would be unclean, but as it is, they are holy. But if the unbeliever leaves, let him do so. A believing man or woman is not bound in such circumstances; God has called us to live in peace. How do you know, wife, whether you will save your husband? Or, how do you know, husband, whether you will save your wife?'

(1 Corinthians 7:12–16)

I often meet Christians who 'for an easy life' want a separation from their unbelieving partner. Some even behave and talk in a way that increases the problems and encourages a divorce. This is sin! Even if problems arise, it must be the unbeliever who refuses to be reconciled. The Christian is exhorted to do all that is possible to hold the marriage together. This is for the unbeliever's sake (that they might come to know Christ) and for the children's sake. However, if the unbelieving partner demands a divorce, the believing partner is not to stand in the way for *'God has called us to live in peace'* (1 Corinthians 7:15). Peter has some wise words that, although addressed to women, do apply to husbands of unbelievers,

> *'Wives, in the same way be submissive to your husbands so that, if any of them do not believe the word, they may be won over without words by the behaviour of their wives, when they see the purity and reverence of your lives.'* (1 Peter 3:1–2)

Many believers hold on for years, refusing a divorce in the hope of reconciliation. However, this often causes more tension, even to the extent of driving the unbeliever to commit adultery.

I often meet Christian women, whose husbands have divorced them and have remarried, who still say, 'I have a word that the Lord will bring him back and we will be together again.' However, as we have already seen, this clearly contradicts God's Word in Deuteronomy 24:1–4.

> *'But if the unbeliever leaves, let him do so. A believing man or woman is not bound in such circumstances.'* (1 Corinthians 7:15)

The word bound, *'douloo'* in the Greek, means to 'be in bondage, to make a slave of'. In other words, for such a person all the bonds and obligations of marriage have been removed. They are now a free person and released to remarry (only a Christian) if they wish.

The Believer with a Believing Partner

> *'To the married I give this command (not I, but the Lord): A wife must not separate from her husband. But if she does, she must remain unmarried or else be reconciled to her husband. And a husband must not divorce his wife.'* (1 Corinthians 7:10–11)

When two married believers are involved, God commands them not to separate. Even if they disobey God's command and part, they are not to remarry; this leaves the door open for repentance and a new start (obviously to marry another would close the door to reconciliation). God's Word gives only one legitimate ground for starting a divorce and that is sexual immorality.

> *'It has been said, "Anyone who divorces his wife must give her a certificate of divorce." But I tell you that anyone who divorces his wife, except for marital unfaithfulness, causes her to become an adulteress, and anyone who marries the divorced woman commits adultry.'*
> (Matthew 5:31–32)

> *'I tell you that anyone who divorces his wife, except for marital unfaithfulness, and marries another woman commits adultery.'* (Matthew 19:9)

The King James Version of the Bible translates marital unfaithfulness as 'fornication'. This has caused some confusion, as the word fornication is now used to mean a sexual sin committed by two unmarried people. However, the Greek word *'porneia'* includes far more than that. It describes incest (1 Corinthians 5:1), homosexuality and other perversions (Jude 7), and adultery (Matthew 19:9). Notice that *porneia* is also the root of a modern word describing another source of marital unfaithfulness – pornography. The Greek word *'moichao'*, translated adultery, also meant unfaithfulness to a marriage partner, but is more specific. Jesus' words, both in Matthew 5 and 19, imply sexual sin of any kind. It was on the grounds of adultery that God divorced Israel (Jeremiah 3:8 and Hosea 2:2).

Although sexual immorality can be the reason for divorce, such action is not always necessary, nor need it be inevitable. If the guilty party will repent, reconciliation can take place, which is far better. God permitted divorce because of man's *'hardness of heart'* (Mark 10:4–5). However, if God is allowed to soften and change a person's heart, even after sexual sin or unfaithfulness, reconciliation is possible.

I always encourage couples wholeheartedly to go for reconciliation; divorce should not be considered if there is any possibility of change. If there is true repentance, the partner must forgive (Matthew 6:14–15). Obviously, if forgiveness is given, any divorce proceedings should stop.

According to Jewish law an adulterer should be stoned to death, which then released the other partner. Jesus gave the adulterous woman another chance (John 8:5). He did not condemn her, but told her to sin no more (John 8:11). Even after acts of unfaithfulness, a partner should always seek to forgive the other, giving them a second chance. Marrying again should never be considered until the door has been finally closed for reconciliation by the partner who has sinned, either by remarriage or death. The Bible is clear that the person is then free to remarry.

Please do not take independent action to divorce or remarry. It is important to talk through these issues with your church leadership and get their covering. If your church teaches something contrary to what I have said in this chapter, please respect and remain committed to your church leaders.

In spite of Israel's sin, God called her back. He made it clear that if she would repent and return, then He would forgive her and take her back. He even took the initiative in seeking her out. She had gone after other lovers, but the Lord said,

> *'I am now going to allure her; I will lead her into the desert and speak tenderly to her.'* (Hosea 2:13–14)

Even after Israel had become a 'prostitute', God said *'return to Me'*, but she refused.

The teaching that adultery automatically dissolves a marriage because 'a new one has been established' is also incorrect. Marriage authorizes sexual relationships, but marriage and sex are not the same thing. If they were, the sin involved would be bigamy not adultery.

New Creatures

Today, many people have already been divorced or re-married before they become Christians. I believe the Bible teaches that God accepts us as we are and has put our past sin *'as far as the east is from the west'* (Psalm 103:12), never to be remembered again! (Hebrews 8:12, see also Hebrews 10:17, Isaiah 38:17, Jeremiah 31:34).

We truly are new creatures,

> *'therefore, if anyone is in Christ, he is a new creation; the old has gone, the new has come!'* (2 Corinthians 5:17)

As for the divorcee, I believe God treats the new Christian as though they were single, and thus free to remarry, providing the door has been closed to reconciliation with their partner. For every married person reading this book you need to settle that you have married for the last time, while you and your partner are both still alive. Believe it, be committed and understand that God is now the third partner of your relationship.

It would be easy to quickly remarry hoping to find healing from the past in a new relationship. However, this can be disastrous. Character faults that contributed to the first breakdown have often been left unchanged and can contribute to a second. An openness for God to deal with any such issue is vital if a future relationship is to work.

Chapter 22

After Things Go Wrong

'You ask, "Why?" It is because the Lord *is acting as the witness between you and the wife of your youth, because you have broken faith with her, though she is your partner, the wife of your marriage covenant. Has not the* Lord *made them one? In flesh and spirit they are his. And why one? Because he was seeking a godly offspring. So guard yourself in your spirit, and do not break faith with the wife of your youth. "I hate divorce," says the* Lord *God of Israel, "and I hate a man's covering himself with violence as well as with his garment," says the* Lord *Almighty. So guard yourself in your spirit, and do not break faith.'* (Malachi 2:14–16)

This is a passage of the Bible that I have often heard people quote; for a long time I did not understand it. Before Heather and I were married, we had to know that what we were planning was in the will of God, and was scriptural. Malachi 2:16 was a verse that puzzled me. Finally I came to the point where I said, 'Lord, what do you mean *"You hate divorce"*'? His reply set me free: 'I hate sin, but I still love the sinner. In the same way, I hate divorce but love the person that is divorced.'

God hates some of the things you do, or have done, but He still loves you. If you are a divorcee, face the reality that God hates divorce, but He does not hate you. He still sent Jesus to die for you. In Christ, your past is irrelevant and you are not condemned (Romans 8:1). Stop condemning yourself and don't let others condemn you. Your past is behind you and you can't do anything to change it. Your Heavenly Father accepts you as you are now.

Billy Graham talking on the subject of divorce and remarriage once said 'You can't unscramble eggs.' That was a real gem of wisdom – God accepts you as you are and you are not to dwell on the past, and what has happened. Live in today.

In Malachi 2, the Lord says something that I believe is very significant for any of us who are in second marriages or are divorced.

> *'Guard yourself in your spirit.'* (Malachi 2:16)

One of the most basic problems we have to face when we are dealing with difficulties in a remarriage is a spirit of bitterness.

> *'See to it that no one misses the grace of God and that no bitter root grows up to cause trouble and defile many.'*
> (Hebrews 12:15)

Often it creeps in so subtly that we don't realise it is there. If you don't deal with it when it appears, that root begins to grow, shoots emerge and can then become an established tree that will overshadow your whole life. Guard **your** spirit, not your partner's. Your bitterness is not his or her fault. Adam blamed God, *'the woman you gave me'* (Genesis 3:12). He had to stand in his own right before God and take the blame for his own sin. We have to do the same.

I think we need to clear the ground so that we can build on something solid and lay a firm foundation for the future. Clearing the ground means we need to face issues and hurts that we have tried to ignore for too long.

> *'Then God said, "Take your son, your only son, Isaac, whom you love, and go to the region of Moriah.*

> *Sacrifice him there as a burnt offering on one of the*
> *mountains I will tell you about.'* (Genesis 22:2)

How many sons did Abraham have? Two, and yet God says *'Take your **only** son.'* Why did God ignore Ishmael? Paul describes him as a child of the flesh in Galatians 4. Isaac, however, was a child of promise by the Spirit of God; he was the child the Lord had planned for Abraham. He produced Ishmael by trying to help God, and in so doing we still see the consequences today in the Arab/Israeli conflict.

God deals very radically with the past when anyone genuinely confesses and repents. You could paraphrase it this way, 'take your wife, your only wife' or 'take your husband, your only husband.' God doesn't hold things against people who repent, so we need to make sure that the past is thoroughly dealt with.

Out of the past come things that we need to clear away if we are going to live harmoniously in the present. I want to look at some of these root issues now, and to start clearing the ground. The issues I want to deal with may all have roots in your past so be open for God to deal with them as you read. But please be real, I meet many people who choose to live in an unreal world, deceiving themselves that they are unaffected by the points that follow. May I encourage you to face these issues and deal with them, you will find a great release in getting free and it will change your future.

Guilt

King David committed adultery with Bathsheba but afterwards he got right with God; that is why God could say that David was a man after His own heart (1 Samuel 13:14). God continued His friendship with David not because he committed adultery but in spite of it. Always remember that God doesn't condone sin. David paid an expensive price but he still came through to God. Look at David's prayer:

> *'Cleanse me with hyssop, and I will be clean; wash me, and I will be whiter than snow. Let me hear joy and gladness; let the bones you have crushed rejoice. Hide your face from my sins and blot out all my iniquity. Create in me a pure heart, O God, and renew a steadfast spirit within me. Do not cast me from your presence or take your Holy Spirit from me. Restore to me the joy of your salvation and grant me a willing spirit, to sustain me.'*
>
> (Psalm 51:7–12)

Isn't that a wonderful prayer? The first thing to note is that David cried out in faith. He believed God could do something. Sadly, many people we meet feel so trapped with guilt that they can't believe that God can free them. Their minds have been put into a legalistic 'straight-jacket', and they seem to live in the 'Condemned Cell'. I feel sad for people like this because all they need to do is pray like David, *'Cleanse me with hyssop, and I will be clean; wash me, and I will be whiter than snow'* (Psalm 51:7).

David goes on, *'Let me hear joy and gladness; let the bones you have crushed rejoice'* (Psalm 51:8). God had given him a hard time but David asked for joy and gladness to come back. *'Hide your face from my sins and blot out all my iniquity'* (Psalm 51:9). God can blot out your sins so they don't exist. David ends his prayer with a great request: *'Create in me a pure heart, O God, and renew a steadfast spirit within me'* (Psalm 51:10). To paraphrase that, David said 'I want You to so change me on the inside, that I will never commit a sin like this again.'

I was once teaching a group of young men, and we were studying the biblical approach to sex. We were studying what the Bible says about the sin of fornication, a biblical word that today means 'sex before marriage'. I said to them, 'If you have committed fornication, repent. Then, in the future, when God allows you to court a young lady, you will not commit the same sin again. That is the sign of true repentance.' Those young men faced that challenge and said how helpful it was to them because sometimes what is

called 'repentance' is wishy-washy and unreal. Some have
prayed 'O Jesus, I committed fornication last night. Please
forgive me and cleanse me in the blood of Jesus. Thank you
for restoring me Lord.' Then next week they are on their
knees, praying the same after sinning again. That is not
repentance. Finney said, 'Godly sorrow works repentance,
never to be repented of again.'

Whatever happens when a marriage breaks down, it is
never just one partner's fault. I did not commit adultery or
anything like that, but there were some very definite defects
in me that contributed to the breakdown of my first marriage. Do not delude yourself that it was 'their fault'. If you
do, you are never really going to change in the way you
need to. Take responsibility and do not make excuses for
what happened.

If you did commit adultery, and in so doing triggered the
break-up of your marriage, you must realise an important
fact. Getting married again does not legalize your sin. You
brought that sin into your new marriage and it will cause
problems until it is dealt with. God works in the light:
Satan works in the darkness! If we hold anything in darkness the devil has a 'landing strip' on which to enter our
lives and cause problems. Thank God that the blood of
Jesus Christ, God's Son, cleanses from all sin; He justifies
us, when we are honest and walk in the light (1 John 1:7).

Condemnation

I often have to counsel folk whom the devil is accusing,
reminding them of sins God has forgiven. The truth is that
there is *no* condemnation for those who are in Christ Jesus.
Until we realise that and believe, Satan will not stop his
accusations. Are you convinced of the truth of Romans
8:1? Whatever anyone says, are you secure in your position
in Christ? You need to know your position in Christ.

Many people have entered a second marriage without
facing the facts of the Word of God. When Heather and I
got married, we spent a long time studying the Word until

we were convinced that we were not breaking one part of it. We knew we could not get married unless we knew beyond any doubt that we were right before God. If you, as a divorcee, are planning to remarry please do make sure that you know the Word. Don't ignore what the Bible says about divorce and remarriage and adultery; go to God and pray it through.

Failure

Failure is a curse many people live with, especially if a marriage has failed in the past. Do you feel incapable of being the husband or the wife you are supposed to be, or that you failed a former partner and let them down? I want you to know that as far as God is concerned He doesn't have any permanent failures. As one of His children, He wants to give you a new start.

In Luke 5 we read the story of Simon Peter who had been fishing all night. He was an experienced fisherman who had worked hard, but caught nothing. Jesus asked to borrow Peter's boat and told him to launch out into the deep water to try again.

> 'Simon answered, "Master, we've worked hard all night and haven't caught anything. But because you say so, I will let down the nets."' (Luke 5:5)

Peter's response gives us the key to getting free from failure. Simply, do what the Lord tells you to do. Whatever the Word of God says, believe it and obey it.

Read Ephesians 5:22–33, Paul's famous passage about marriage. If you read on into chapter 6, Paul talks about being good parents to your children. Note that there is no distinction made whether they are from a previous marriage or not. Every child will respond to the real thing in the end, but you need to start with the Word. Don't try to make excuses by saying 'You don't know my children.' God made our children and He made them to respond to love.

226

There is hope and I want you to be aware of that hope right now. You may have remarried but you do not now have a second class marriage or family life. However much failure there has been in the relationship between you and the children, you must believe that there is hope. Come back to the Word, put your marriage and your parenthood on clear biblical principles and it will work. You are not a failure, God will give you victory.

Low Self-worth

I often hear people confess 'I am no good' or 'I will never be a good wife (or good husband), I have this "past".' It's sad but sometimes because of marriage failure, the Church sows seeds that produce low self-esteem and low self-worth in people. Don't accept that. To be a good husband or a good wife you must believe that you are one, because God has given you the ability to become the best. I always tell people that Heather is the best wife in the world, and I honestly believe it. She is the best wife in the world for me. There is no other person in the whole world who could be the kind of wife that I need. She is God's gift. He gave her to me.

Sometimes Heather says 'Don, you are the best husband in the world.' When she does I do not respond 'Don't be so silly, there are better people than me.' If she says I'm the best husband, she is the one who should know! I'm not going to spend the rest of my life arguing with her. I believe it. I don't believe I'm better than others, I just believe that I'm the best for her. God gave me to her. On the 9th May 1964 I stood before God and said 'I will take this woman to be my wife.' God sealed it and now we belong to each other; no one is going to take us away from each other.

You need to understand how much you are worth to the Lord. Let's illustrate this with football players. Many millions of pounds are paid each year for men who can play football well. In comparison God paid far more than five million pounds to get me. He paid an incredible amount to transfer me from the kingdom of Satan to the Kingdom of His dear Son. The price was the life of His Son; that is what I am worth to God.

'He has made us accepted in the Beloved.'
(Ephesians 1:6)

'You are His, and He takes you on just as you are.'
(Romans 14:7)

'Accept one another, then, just as Christ accepted you, in order to bring praise to God.' (Romans 15:7)

If I take these verses seriously what must I do? Simply accept Heather and take her just as Christ accepted her. I know she accepts and takes me the same way too. How did Christ accept you? Did He say, 'Don, if you improve yourself, and you stop doing this and you stop doing that, I'll take you on?' No! He said, 'I'll take you, just as you are (warts and all).'

I have been asked to officiate at several weddings, and one of the conditions I insist upon is that the couple do a course in marriage preparation. (See the appendix at the back of this book for an outline.) If I take the course, the first thing I get them to do is to give each other a good look. Then I ask a very simple question: 'Are you prepared to spend the rest of your life with this person, without them ever changing? If you are not, don't get married!' It sounds blunt, but it is important that 'love' doesn't cloud the issue. Several couples have been unable to answer this question and have cancelled the wedding; one in spite of invitations already sent out and a dress bought.

I believe that the only way you are allowed to change your partner is to pray for them. When the Bible talks to wives, it means husbands mind your own business, and when it says husbands, it means wives mind your own business. Too many wives spend all their lives trying to make their husbands better, so much so that they never quite become a good wife, and vice versa. Find out what God says about you and work at that. Seek to become a good partner. The best way I have found of changing Heather is to get my part right. Then I do all I can to fulfil all that God's word says about being a good husband.

Rejection

A marriage break-down can produce the worst kind of rejection in a person. From my own experience I know the pain of this rejection. A long time after my first marriage was over I thought I had come through it, but years later I was still reacting to things because of that rejection. I needed deliverance, some cleaning up of the root issue.

One of the things you can't do when you are rejected, is trust. No marriage can work to its full potential where there is no trust. Before I married Heather, I said I would never trust a woman again. Thank God He delivered me. I now am able to trust Heather anywhere, and with anyone. Trust has to be built up, it is not something that drops out of the sky. Get free from your rejection and then start to build trust.

Selfishness

Selfishness is a major cause of marriage breakdown. If you bring the problem that caused your first marriage to break down into your second, the same problems will occur. Therefore, if you have not allowed God to change you, don't be surprised if you find yourself in similar situations.

When it comes to selfishness, often the first thing to recognise is that the motives for marrying someone may be wrong. Why did you marry? Think that question through. If you had, or still have a wrong motive, face it, repent and ask God to change your attitude.

Another root of selfishness can be a sense of competitiveness. Many marriages have broken down because partners are competing in some way. If there is any way in which you are competing against each other, be careful. Marriage needs a husband and wife to be a team, working and pulling together. Instead of 'partnership', I like to use the word 'harmony', because, as we have set out in earlier chapters, a man and a woman have completely different roles. We each bring our contribution and the two come into harmony. Personally, I think the best sounds you ever hear in music are harmonies. That is what a good marriage is, a harmony; each brings individual gifts that together make something better and more pleasing.

So often selfishness can be a major cause of sexual problems, as partners seek self-satisfaction. I believe the Bible shows that all sexual intercourse should always seek to fulfil and satisfy the other partner. If you get that right there is every chance it will help to develop a good, harmonious relationship.

How do you deal with selfishness? There is only one way and that is to come to the cross. For all the things I have mentioned above, the answer is the cross of Jesus. If both of you understand the potential blessing that came through the death of Jesus Christ it will play a very valuable contribution to the success of your marriage. Guilt, condemnation, failure, low self-esteem, rejection and selfishness, are all dealt with completely by the cross. Paul says,

> *'May I never boast except in the cross of our Lord Jesus Christ, through which the world has been crucified to me, and I to the world.'*   (Galatians 6:14)

> *'I have been crucified with Christ and I no longer live, but Christ lives in me. The life I live in the body, I live by faith in the Son of God, who loved me and gave himself for me.'*   (Galatians 2:20)

If you are struggling with any of the issues I have talked about in this chapter, spend some time praying with your partner. Review the points I have raised and the scriptures

I have used. Then agree together that the Word and the power of the Holy Spirit will change you. Look forward to a relationship and a family life better than ever before.

Chapter 23

Children in a Second Marriage

When I married Don, I was a single person marrying a divorcee. As a result, we faced some advantages and some disadvantages compared to two single people marrying. For instance, Don had experience of running a home. We didn't make many mistakes in setting up a home because he had done that before and we were able to avoid some of the pitfalls that many young married people get into.

There were also some disadvantages. I married a man who had known sexual fulfilment and so there was not the excitement of discovery together. The danger came in making comparisons, judging against what he had known or experienced before. Anyone who is remarrying needs to settle this issue as it has a critical effect on your relationship. God has made us all different. Because of that our sexual experiences are going to be different. Every sexual relationship is unique before God, so don't compare. Whatever your previous sexual experiences, come to your marriage determined to start anew. Even the petting and stimulation you enjoyed before has to be put behind you; realise that what stimulates one person does not necessarily stimulate another person. It is important to talk about this with your partner and work it out.

Another disadvantage that I felt was that I had to live up to someone else, to another person's lifestyle. I felt I was being compared to the way Don's former wife had done things. Sometimes when people first get married you hear the partner saying, 'My mother did it this way' or 'mother never did that.' For people who remarry not only is there the 'mother' syndrome, but also the 'first wife' or 'first husband' syndrome.

Getting married marks a fresh start. I suggest that a lot of problems can be avoided by starting a completely new lifestyle together. When Don and I counsel someone who is remarrying, we suggest they follow the pattern we worked out between us.

We were very fortunate, when Don and I married, we travelled for most of each year; it was several years before we actually started our own home together. We began from scratch, with no furniture, no mementoes, nothing to do with former relationships. Our recommendation is that you do the same. Many problems are caused by attachment to memories in the home, to possessions, to furniture, to things that need to be got out of the way. Financially it may be a hard decision to get rid of so much, but God will honour you if it is for the good of your relationship. Hanging on to old experiences, to sentimental feelings, won't help living today, however good they seem.

There was a time when I felt I was always being compared; I think that is inevitable in any second marriage. It does not matter how spiritual you are, nor how much ministry you have had, there is always a danger of being compared with a previous relationship. I felt I needed to be myself, to be accepted for who I was, not for what Don wanted me to be. You need to watch out for this very carefully in each other.

Many of the principles we teach in this book will work, no matter what 'number' marriage you are in. If you are faithful to God's Word I believe He will be faithful to you and you will see a change in your family. However, there are some specific issues that parents with children from another marriage need to address.

I have what the world would call two stepchildren, but I have never ever considered them as that, and don't like to use the title 'stepchildren'. It does not matter how they came to you – children are a gift from God. Whether they came naturally, by adoption, by fostering, or by getting married to a person who has already had children, they are still God's gift to you.

Before I got married to Don I have to admit that I didn't really get on with children. When they were around us, children always seemed to gravitate to my brother; in a sense I didn't have time for children. Yet the moment I started courting Don, God gave me a real love for his two children because they were a part of him. I started to love them because they were part of the person I loved. I know that God only gives me good gifts (Matthew 7:11), therefore children, as a gift from God, are a blessing.

So, Don and I married and immediately I was a mother to two children, Nigel who was eight and Julia who was five. We had to establish a relationship and my first goal was to befriend them. Before I tried to have any authority in their lives I had to 'win' them. Although they were quite young, they had been hurt, and had learnt to distrust; I needed to start building a relationship in which they could start to trust me. It took some time and initially it was hard work, but I needed to understand them emotionally.

Children who have lost a parent, for whatever reason, do have an awareness of what has happened. When a change occurs, like the appearance of a 'new' parent, it is going to take time for them to adjust. It is likely that one thought that they will have is: 'Is this person going to do the same as my own mother or father? Are they going to betray me and walk out?' They might not express these thoughts in words, but children do think this way 'underneath'. They are uncertain of your love for them as individuals and you need to give them time to learn to trust again.

A serious fear some children have is that the new parent has stolen their father's or mother's affection. The one secure thing that they had left was the remaining parent. Now there is another person who has appeared and says they love Mum or Dad. This can be a terrible threat to them and if you are the 'intruder' you really need to be sensitive in handling their reactions.

In a new situation, the children of previous marriages are likely to be very cautious, perhaps feeling betrayed and insecure. When you are trying to establish a friendship it can be a big barrier to get over, but stick at it. If you also have been through a divorce you may feel the same way. I strongly encourage you to get that sorted out quickly, before you try to build with your children. If you too are hurt you can risk adding to their hurt.

A major cause of continuing pain and tension can be the 'visit'. Regularly they go off to visit their other natural parent for a weekend, or sometimes for a holiday. Then they come back to you. While this 'access' can be a positive experience, often it leaves children feeling torn in two. They don't know how to relate to either parent. Many experience this with four 'parents' and do not know how to handle it. Start helping them through it, don't get threatened but as the old phrase goes, 'be part of the solution, don't be part of the problem.'

Despite past hurts and events it is crucial that you build a respect into them for the person who gave them life.

> *'Honour your father and your mother, so that you may live long in the land the LORD your God is giving you.'*
> (Exodus 20:12)

The Word of God must override all other considerations and that means you need to teach your children to respect their natural parents. However, as your relationship develops with the child, make sure they honour their mother and father.

As you build a friendship, a big factor in it is learning to be sensitive. As mentioned earlier, in a second marriage there is always the tendency to compare and it happens with the children as much as with the adults. For instance, there may have been something special that Dad used to do with them, perhaps reading them a story when they went to bed at night. The child might not want you to do that with them, because it is a reminder of the past. Don't feel obliged to 'press through with it'. Forget it for a while, and don't force them to do things you think they should do. Try to talk the issue through with them, drawing out what they feel. 'Why don't you like doing that with me?' Give the child some 'space' to work out what he feels and then encourage him then to put the past behind.

Although you may find this difficult, I would suggest that you leave the issue of discipline to the natural parent. Your priority is to build a friendship. A great help in this is to find something that they can teach you. For all my children it has been a major part of becoming friends. With our son Joel it was computers. I didn't know anything about them, but he had been given one for Christmas and he was having great fun with it. I asked him to teach me how they worked and it really did something for our relationship. Some people think there is nothing their children can teach them. The truth is that our children are learning things at school we never did and they are technologically far more aware than we are.

There will always be something that they can teach you. With my daughter Faith, it was pop music. She really enjoyed it and so I used to watch 'Top of the Pops' with her. We would discuss the lyrics, the music and everything. One benefit from that is that I can trust her with what she listens to. The moment she recognises something is wrong or unhealthy she will switch it off.

When I talk about being a friend to your children, I remember one lady who reacted, 'I will never be her friend because I am her mother!' That is sad, because it shows a very narrow understanding of what a mother's role is. With young children, discipline and authority are important parts of the relationship. But that is not the end of it – believe that the discipline you bring will be effective and you will produce a person able to control themselves. What then? Many parents fail to see that they need to develop the relationship with their children further. As each of my children got into senior school I sought to befriend them. When relating to stepchildren, or those who have been adopted or fostered it is even more important this happens.

Don't allow your children, whatever their relationship to you, ever to come between you and your partner. God has made you, husband and wife, as one; don't let the children divide you. If you sense it happening, get together and talk it through. If an issue comes up that you disagree with your partner about, don't disagree in front of the children. Never let the children see that you are divided, but make sure that they see that you are one.

Grieving and Brokenness

> *'The spirit of a man will sustain him in sickness, But who can bear a broken spirit?'* (Proverbs 18:14 NKJV)

> *'A merry heart makes a cheerful countenance, But by sorrow of the heart the spirit is broken.'*
> (Proverbs 15:13 NKJV)

Broken families will produce children with broken spirits. We need to do something about it, although it often feels that we are helpless to do anything. I always had the idea that grief was something associated with death. I never thought about grief in any other context. My only experiences of relatives dying, were of Christians and so there was no real mourning. I had an understanding of grieving that did not really touch me.

Then one Sunday morning the Lord really spoke to me about a broken relationship. It was not a marriage relationship, but someone who had recently broken off our friendship. The Lord showed me that I was grieving although I didn't realise it. My 'subconscious' grief had made me hard inside and I had decided that I was not going to let anyone else hurt me. No-one would have a close relationship with me because I was not going to get hurt again. It all started because I was grieving over a broken relationship, and it shocked me.

From the experiences Don and I have had counselling people, I would expect that many people who are divorced, and are reading this book, are still grieving. You might not put it in those terms but you are. In your spirit there is still grief over what happened in your previous marriage. You need to finish grieving because until it is over it will hinder any new relationships you try to establish. You may need to receive ministry to get that grief out before you can really start building with someone else, especially in the area of building with children.

A major release from grief comes simply through tears. In our culture we have an odd attitude to crying. Boys especially are told that it is not part of being 'grown-up' and mature. We need to refute that idea and see that God made tears for a purpose. Crying is an important method of expressing your emotions.

When we were in Israel a few years ago I learnt something that has been very precious to me. There were two passages in the Bible that I had struggled to understand. In Psalm 56:8 it says that God keeps our tears in His bottle. Why would God do that? Then in the New Testament it says that Mary washed Jesus' feet with her tears. I can remember as a teenager thinking she must have cried a lot. It takes a big bowl of water to wash a man's size nine feet that are sandy and dusty. How did she do that? She must have cried for a long time.

We were on the Mount of Olives looking over Old Jerusalem and the Temple Site. On the Mount of Olives are several churches and one of them is supposedly on the site where Jesus cried over Jerusalem (Luke 19:41). All around the grounds of the church are tall bottles, with wide tops, very narrow necks, and great big bowls at the bottom. Our guide explained their purpose: A Jewish woman never cries in public and she never wipes away her tears. She has a 'tear bottle' which she cries into and keeps her tears. The big bottles are a place for storing the tears! The guide went on to explain the significance of Mary's encounter with Jesus as she washed Jesus' feet. She used those tears she had collected. It is possible to conclude that she had led a life full of grief to have had so many tears. I think it is a beautiful picture of how Jesus can deal with our grief and the things that cause it.

Psalm 56 took on a new meaning for me. God keeps our tears in His bottle. He remembers every grief that you have; it says in Isaiah 53 that Jesus was acquainted with our grief. He knows what it is to grieve. We need to experience grief's release in tears, letting the emotion out. It doesn't matter what relationship is involved, release that grief, so that we can allow other people into our lives and encourage them to do the same.

In Conclusion

The writer of Ecclesiastes, after covering many issues of life, concludes what he has to say with comments that concern the fear of God and keeping His commandments.

> 'Let us hear the conclusion of the whole matter: Fear God and keep His commandments, For this is man's all. For God will bring every work into judgment, Including every secret thing, Whether good or evil.'
>
> (Ecclesiastes 12:13–14 NKJV)

When it comes to marriage and following the 'Maker's Instructions' as God intended, we must remember that it was His idea in the first place. He knows best how to make it work. The blueprint for marriage was indeed made in heaven. But, marriages are not – they have to be worked out on earth. Husband and wife both need to be dedicated to building together. How?

The most basic step is to fear the God who made marriage. The fear of the Lord is more powerful than having faith in God. A good marriage should be founded on a healthy respect for God, that He knows best. If we think we know it all and try to leave God out we will miss it.

Having read this book you now have to put the principles you have learnt into practice. Remember that Jesus taught His followers that if we hear the word of God and don't do it, it is like building on sand. When the pressure comes anything we have built will collapse. If we follow the 'Maker's Instructions' we will build on solid rock that provides a strong foundation. Even 'gale force storms' won't move a marriage with God's foundations.

Don't give up when things get tough. God is faithful and His way works. It may cost you a lot in pride and effort to change, but the results will be worthwhile. You are not on your own – He will give grace and strength to enable everyone of us to go on. **Keep Going!**

For further information about the ministry of Evangelist Don Double and the Good News Crusade please write to:

Good News Crusade
17 High Cross Street
ST AUSTELL
Cornwall
PL25 4AN

Appendix

Preparing to Get Married

Most people who read this book will already be married; probably at some point in reading, you have said 'I wish someone had told me that before I got married!' This appendix has been included to help those who are planning to get married in the near future.

When I agree to officiate at someone's wedding I insist that there is some preparation done beforehand. If I am to do that I usually take six sessions with the couple, leading up to the 'big day'. I encourage them to pray and discuss the things we talk about before the next session, and I recommend a book for them to read. I suggest that they read and discuss it together. At the next session they can then tell me what they have learnt from the book; also it is useful to provoke the couple to deal with many of the issues we have raised in this book and start them asking questions about things they must face.

I always recommend that any couple considering marriage go to the minister who will marry them and ask for some marriage preparation. If he or she is unable or unwilling to do that, I would suggest the couple find a local Christian ministry that is; it is really important and should be a high priority in the plans for the wedding. The information that follows is necessarily general but does cover most of the areas an engaged couple need to consider. In the rest of this chapter I will address my remarks to the couple:

Session 1

Planning

I want you to realise that you are entering a covenant. I am assuming that you are both committed Christians and know that what you are doing is done in the light of God's word. Marriage is a final, irrevocable, permanent commitment; divorce should not be an option for you.

Now I want you to turn and take a good look at each other. Ask yourselves this question as honestly as you can:

'Do you want to spend the rest of your life with this person?'

If the answer is 'Yes' then, Hallelujah! Let's get ready for the wedding. **But**, if the answer is 'No', Hallelujah! We have prevented a broken marriage. It does not matter how far in the planning you have got – if you cannot say that you are willing to live with this person for the rest of your life **do not** get married. This step is likely to be painful and awkward, but far less so than the agony of a broken marriage.

If the answer is 'Not sure' we need to talk through the reasons for being hesitant. It may mean you will have to go away to consider your future and then meet again to decide on your answer. But, however long it takes no couple should get married unless they can both answer yes to the question.

Be aware that there are a number of people who have answered 'No' when asked the question; you will not be the first to break the engagement. Also, you need to be aware that it is easier for the man to say no than the woman, especially if plans are already under way and money has been spent. However, I would underline that it is far better to stop now, despite some loss of pride and money rather than face far more unhappiness and grief later on. Don't let people fool you into thinking divorce is 'painless'. Every divorce creates damaged people.

Planning the Wedding Day

'Any old thing' will not do. Your wedding day should be very memorable – a day that will bring pleasant memories and be a strong influence upon you for the rest of your lives together.

The bridegroom-to-be, should fully understand that it is the bride's 'big day'. Therefore, you should do everything you can to make it a wonderful day for your wife. Both of you should begin to plan, pray and share your desires for the day together. It should be an exciting time as you share together in making decisions about the wedding. For most people it is the biggest party you will ever throw, and everyone will be there because of you so make sure that you can enjoy it.

Things you need to think about include:

The type of service you want. Only a small part of the 'official ceremony' is the legal part. You should be free to celebrate your marriage in the way you want. That will obviously affect the 'Order of service' and what hymns and other songs you choose. Before you talk to the person officiating at the wedding, talk about what each other wants, and don't necessarily conform to the ritual and tradition of your church. For instance should you take Communion together during the service?

At this point you will need to decide who should participate in the actual marriage service. That includes bridesmaids – discuss how many you want and who you will ask.

You need to discuss and decide how you are going to remember the day. Will it be videoed? Do you want a photographer as well? Personally I think it is important to arrange for the best photographer you can afford, so that you have a really good album at the end – it is an expensive item, but a worthwhile investment.

Then you need to decide about the reception. What kind of reception is it to be and who do you invite? Who would you like to share and speak at the reception?

Parents

Fashions change; it used to be the Bride's parents who decided most of the above, but today the couple themselves are far more involved. However, don't ignore or exclude your parents, it is a big day for them as well. Equally don't be persuaded into doing things you don't want. Weddings can be a time of fraught family relationships, but that can be avoided by being committed to talk things through. I suggest that if possible, you arrange for an evening that the two of you can get both sets of parents together to talk and plan together.

Finally there is the wedding present list to decide upon and get circulating. Don't be afraid or embarrassed to ask for big presents like washing machines.

To the Bride

As an act of love, in seeking to please your future husband, discreetly find out what type of dress he really likes. Should there be lots of lace or brocade; does he prefer a long or shorter dress? Should the veil be long or short? (In the same way, the groom should discover the type of suit the bride likes.)

Planning the Honeymoon

I believe it is good to have the best honeymoon possible, even if it means a sacrifice. I am aware the everyone has their own desires regarding the perfect holiday and honeymoon but I would like to give some advice. If possible have a honeymoon in a warm climate, and choose somewhere where you are unlikely to meet anybody you know, so that you can really be on your own.

On your return, it is advisable, if possible to have an additional week in your new home so that you can learn to live together before going back to work.

Planning the New Home

The Bible teaches the sanctity of the family. Therefore I

believe every married couple should share their life together in a home of their own, however simple it might be, even if it is only two rooms.

The principle we have explained in detail in this book is that *'For this reason a man shall leave his father and mother'* (your parents must also let go), to begin a new life together with the husband as the head of the home and the wife in submission to him. It is so essential that you start your life on your own, away from your in-laws. I think you should seriously consider postponing the wedding if you are unable to find somewhere on your own immediately.

A true home is somewhere where there is love. It is far more than bricks and furniture. You will find yourselves able to express your love to each other in a far more wonderful way as you begin life together. Use your time together to the maximum, to pray and share together, building good, solid and deep foundation in your relationships, so that it is unshakeable when pressures come along.

Recommended book: *The Marriage Covenant* by Derek Prince.

Session 2

Relationships

One of the important things to realize is that, as yet, you do not really know each other, no matter how long you have been courting. Many times as I counsel young couples on this vital subject they have smiled at me disbelievingly. The truth is that no-one can really know another until they have begun to live together. There are still many things to discover about each other.

Keep your relationship clean, keep right with God and each other. Keep short accounts with God and ask each other for forgiveness whenever it is necessary, as soon as possible.

It is vital that you do not get married with the idea that you are going to change each other. Unless you can love each other whatever you discover about your partner, I would seriously suggest that you call the marriage off before it is too late.

You must be willing to accept each other as you are. It is so important to share your hearts at the very deepest level, being open and not wearing a mask or trying to be someone else. Perhaps you have a picture in your mind of the kind of person you think your partner would really like to have married and so you try to live like that image. This will not work – be yourself.

The vast majority of marriage problems start with poor communication. If you have not thought about this before get a recommended book on the subject, read it and discuss it together. Seek to 'open up' to each other, so that there are no secrets between you. I would strongly recommend that you read chapters 4 and 5 of this book alongside this session.

It is important before the wedding day to regularly pray, seek God and read His Word together. Endeavour to both have the same spiritual desires and hunger for God in your lives so that you can both pull in the same direction.

Again I would emphasize the importance of playing your correct role in the family. The Maker's Instructions are clear, and guarantee the best results!

Recommended book: *Communication, Sex & Money* by Edwin Louis Cole.

Session 3

Economics

Finance has been at the root of many marriage problems and the cause of some breaking up. Therefore it is important to plan and talk through on this subject long before you are married. It is essential for you to hold the same goals economically.

A saying that is often quoted is, 'when the bills come in through the door, love flies out through the window.'

Undue pressures can come into your marriage relationships because of finance. It is better to go without some items of furniture than to have hire purchase repayments that you cannot afford, which can bring pressures upon the financial position of the home. There is tremendous joy to be received through saving up for an item and then going together to buy it, paying cash (and very likely receiving a good cash discount), far more than having everything at once on HP. Often, by the time it is paid for, it is worn out or at the best in secondhand condition.

For example, it would be better to go without a television set than to have it on HP and find pressure in paying instalments or rental. In fact, I strongly advise couples not to have a television set in the first year of married life. It can be such a hindrance to sharing together and building a good strong relationship. It is essential to plan what you can and what you cannot afford. Live well within your means, so that you have spare cash to live with comfortably each week.

It is also very important to see that when you are married every part of you should become one – this includes your finances. Many problems are caused in marriage by the husband saying, 'This is mine' and the wife retaliating with, 'That is mine.' When we marry it should become our money. There should be only one account shared by both husband and wife. You are one now and whatever you have or receive automatically becomes 'ours'.

Independence was the first sin. It is still sin, yet our modern society tends to teach independence in marriage, which is very destructive.

Recommended book: As for Session 2.

Session 4

Sexual relationships

This is a vital part of any marriage relationship and rightly so. Most couples preparing for marriage are looking forward to this aspect very much indeed. God created sexual relationships as part of His plan for our lives. Therefore, within marriage it is wholesome and good. The husband needs to realize that it is his responsibility to satisfy his wife and bring her to a full climax; the wife should similarly seek to fully satisfy her husband and make this her main motive in the relationship. In sexual relationships, selfishness is sin and destructive. Whether it is being demanding or unresponsive, both are a display of selfishness.

Intercourse should not be used as a means of bargaining to get your own way. Freely discuss your sexual relationships, especially sharing the things that you enjoy most, the things you can respond to and any 'hang-ups' you have. Discussing problems openly is probably 90% of conquering them. God intends our sex life to be exciting and adventurous. We need to be liberated from the concept that intercourse is limited to 10 pm at night, in bed with the lights out! Another practical thing to discuss is how often you expect to make love. At this point that may seem an odd statement but being honest about your desires and expectations with each other can avoid frustration and miscommunication later on.

Television can destroy successful relationships. This is an area where we need real discipline. Many couples sit up so late at night watching TV that they get overtired. Sexual relationships do not work right when we are overtired.

Be wary of the many negative seeds sown by other people, including relatives and even parents. Comments like 'Oh, it soon wears off after the honeymoon' or 'There is nothing very much in it' are often made. I would say, as one who has been married for many years that it never wears off, it gets better as your relationship matures! One dear couple, who regularly worked with us celebrated their Golden Wedding anniversary and said that they were as much in love as on the day they got married. They declared that their relationship was still growing, maturing and getting better. God says,

> *'May your fountain be blessed, and may you rejoice in the wife of your youth. A loving doe, a graceful deer – may her breasts satisfy you always, may you ever be captivated by her love.'* (Proverbs 5:19)

There is another bad seed that can be sown, the effect of which is not often realized, but can take root in the heart of a wife. The comment is, 'Oh, there is nothing in it for the wife; only the husband gets anything out of sex.' This is so very wrong. There is just as much for the wife as for the husband in their sexual relationship together. God created us and He did not create us so that one would receive more pleasure than the other. Therefore, reject any of these negative seeds.

One of the most important things to do is to read a good Christian book (and I stress that it should be written by Christians) on the subject. One which I strongly recommend is *Intended for Pleasure* by Ed and Gaye Wheat. This should be read by the couple about a month before the actual date of the wedding. After the wedding day, it is good to keep it in the home as a 'text' book that you can refer to at any time.

Additional recommended books: *The Touch of Love* by John and Janet Houghton; *The Act of Marriage* by Tim and Beverly LaHaye.

Session 5

The Family

I would normally recommend that it is good for a couple to wait, if possible, at least two years before starting a family. Having said that there are other considerations that may mean you want to start a family earlier, for instance a couple who are in their thirties and feel there is 'not much time left' to start a family. My reason for suggesting a period of waiting is so that you can have plenty of time to get to know and to enjoy each other and begin to build a good strong family home for a baby to be born into. It will take those two years to make the necessary adjustments in life, for, as soon as the baby arrives there will be new adjustments to make.

This then raises the whole matter of birth control, on which there are many different and varied views. There is certainly nothing unscriptural about it. The Bible makes no specific comments about the use of birth control methods. However, 'family planning' is an aid to the success of your marriage. It prevents overloading a family with too many children too quickly, and also releases the couple from the fear of an 'untimely' child. If it is possible, I suggest every couple talk to a Christian doctor about the methods which are godly and advisable.

Session 6

Final preparations

In the final session I briefly go over all the points covered before, reminding them of the principles and answering any questions.

If I am officiating the wedding, we will then go through the service and usually this will involve a rehearsal in the building, together with everyone else who is contributing to the service.

I teach them on the importance of praying and reading God's Word together every day and establishing family devotions. I suggest that they make it a really good and lively time together. One of the most beautiful memories of my honeymoon is when Heather and I got to our destination, before we went to bed, kneeling together and reading God's Word and praying together.

At the end of this session I suggest that we meet together a little while after they have got back home and settled into their routine. It is an opportunity to raise any questions or problems that have occurred, and is also a chance to make sure things are OK.